I0210205

Love, Explained

Love, Explained

Practical Strategies to Find and Keep the Love You Deserve, from the Science of Love and Affection

Scott Marshall

Copyright © 2017 by Scott Marshall

All rights reserved. This book or any portion thereof may not be reproduced or used in any manner whatsoever without the express written permission of the author except for the use of brief quotations in a book review.

First U.S. Edition 2017

ISBN: 978-0-9994506-0-4 (softcover)
ISBN: 978-0-9994506-1-1 (hardcover)
ISBN: 978-0-9994506-2-8 (ebook)

Library of Congress Control Number: 1-5829428081

Illustrative anecdotes describe actual events, but participants' names were changed to protect their identities and respect their privacy.

Created on chromebooks with Google Docs.
Set in Libre Baskerville, Trebuchet MS, and Syncopate.
Cover design by Kip Rosser.

FOR PENELOPE

Contents

Acknowledgements

Everyone I've been close to collectively and individually gave me lessons through shared experiences that contributed to the ideas in this book. In the five years from when the ideas here were conceived to the final rewrite, a number of friends have been more directly helpful—the ones who didn't immediately change the subject when I told them I was writing a book about love. A few were interested and eager to help. Friends I really appreciate for believing in me include Sharna and Laura, Susan G. and Brad, and Stephen and Bertrand. Jonathan Goldstein, a business consultant I see frequently for breakfast and table tennis, was very supportive with many ideas to help clarify the book's thesis, shape its structure, and strategize its publication. My son, Leigh, an English teacher, critiqued and edited an early draft, and my friend Jonathan Allen was the first to volunteer to read all the way through one of the final drafts, making helpful suggestions for improvements.

Preface

I don't like mysteries. Though I'm attracted to and enchanted by them, I feel compelled to solve them, even if the consequence is to lose some of that feeling of wonder of the unsolved mystery. I was once asked in a getting-acquainted game: "What's your superpower?" Some people are great at cooking, decorating their homes, finding bargains, throwing parties, meeting new friends—whatever their remarkable hobby or talent is. I answered that some thought I could fix anything, and the response was: "Can you fix a broken heart?" I took this as a challenge. It excited me. Understanding the mechanics of feelings has been a common thread in my career, and my confidence that we are complicated biological machines, and a lot like simpler animals, led me to attack the subject enthusiastically and optimistically. This book is the result of that endeavor—to know what love is, how love works, and, hopefully, to mend our broken hearts.

While binging on author/biology professor Robert Sapolsky's "Human Behavioral Biology" lectures, I was intrigued by a moment in his talk about the connection between how women choose perfumes and the functions and consequences of human pheromones—the chemicals we naturally excrete to communicate with each other, consciously and unconsciously, by smell. A student raised his hand and asked a question, unfortunately unintelligible because of microphone placement, to which Sapolsky responded with an offhanded comment that his students were now concocting dating strategies based on what he'd been teaching them about human biology. That was the *aha* moment that initiated this book—how scientific knowledge can help us to love and better understand each other—to put the theory of love into practice.

Why isn't this book written by a psychologist, psychotherapist, marriage counselor, or philosopher? Perhaps a novel insight is not as likely to come from those following conventional thought, from inside the establishment, than from outside those professions. Indeed, what I've read or been told by relationship experts and pundits has proven of little use to me, and a search of the literature similarly made evident the dearth of new and useful ideas on how to succeed in loving relationships. Isaac Newton said, "If I have seen further, it is by standing on the shoulders of giants." If, however, these giants of ancient wisdom in the theory of love, from Plato to Freud to Fromm, were looking in the wrong direction, then standing on their shoulders only magnified their errors. The original version of the shoulders of giants idea goes back hundreds of years before Newton and had to do with building on previous discoveries. It's the discoveries in the *biology* of love that have made the greatest contributions to the ideas of this book and inspired a unified theory that will help us to master the art of human connection.

Introduction

Why would you want to keep love mysterious if you could use the knowledge of how love actually worked, to become a more effectively loving person? Indeed, how could you do *anything* well if you didn't understand it, but instead considered it a deep and unyielding mystery?

Some friends I told I was writing a book to demystify love stopped me from discussing it further, claiming they wanted it to remain mysterious. We get pleasure, a feeling of enchantment, from mysteries. Wanting to keep something a mystery has to do with the fear of losing the pleasure, since we know, from experience, that when a mystery is solved, it can be disappointing in two ways: The enchantment of the mystery is lost, and the solution can sometimes be less interesting than what we'd hoped for. We know from experience that learning how a magician's trick is done is often a let-down. We like the possibility, for instance, that someone has the magic power to make a rabbit appear and disappear in and out of thin air. It's a disappointment to find the rabbit was just hidden in the magician's coat, and it's painful to acknowledge we'd made a rather silly assumption. We don't always *want* to know that behind the smoke, fire, and fury of an all-powerful wizard is just a shy, insecure man hiding simple gimmicks behind a curtain. We suffer a loss. The trick becomes mundane. It is "reduced" from being a cosmic enchantment to mere mechanics.

My promise is, when something we do is demystified, we can be better at it. Would you want someone you asked to repair your air conditioning to think its workings were completely mysterious? What if your car repairman had no idea how an engine worked? We sacrifice, by keeping something mysterious, competence and mastery. As much pleasure as we get from keeping love a mystery, the tradeoff is to compromise our ability to be good at it. To not be good at love is to leave us unable to begin new relationships, maintain existing ones, restore those that are failing—and to not know why. We will likely fail to find someone whose love will enrich us, and fail to love others well. What we should ask ourselves is why something so important to living life to the fullest, indeed making life worthwhile, should remain mysterious, when the promise of demystifying it could have enormous yield? The promise here is that the loss of that enchanting intrigue of love's "mystery" will be more than compensated for by the gain in *competency*—to love better, and therefore to be loved more. It's worth it.

Love is often wondrous and powerful. It feels like an overwhelming cosmic force that connects us to the whole of the universe. We are baffled by its seeming complexity as it lifts us to the heights of ecstasy, then throws us into crushing despair.

The classical Greek philosophers acknowledged what they felt were four distinct types of love—charity, passion, friendship, and affection—but hardly delved into the common thread that linked them, which we'll do here. That common thread is the keystone principle of this book. The philosophers, from the ancients to those of the present, went off the rails because their cultures developed their ideas before the biological foundations were discovered. What is persistently mysterious is likely just persistently misunderstood. Ever since I first fell under the spell of romantic "puppy love" in middle school at about age thirteen, love has been a mystery to me. It is among the handful of great mysteries of existence. It's time to start the demystification!

Love's basis is nature. We are a part of nature and are related to all life forms on Earth. And they all embody the essential principles of love.

This book is not about sex, though love and sex are related, and it's not necessarily about romance. It's about all kinds of love and all kinds of affection. Not just love for romantic partners, but also for our children, parents, siblings, coworkers, neighbors, and nearly everything else we use the word for. The different kinds of love are variations on a single theme, like different covers of the same song. But, since this book offers a novel perspective on the subject, it requires that we revise the very meaning of the "L" word. We could coin a new word, but that would seem futile. We are discussing what is commonly regarded as love, so let's adjust the definition to align it better with its deeper biological reality.

This is a science book, a nature book, and a how-to book. Its intent is to uncover the principles of how love works, to support those principles with real-life examples as well as explanations from

9

behavioral biology, and to suggest practical strategies to master our ability to create, maintain, and restore loving relationships of all types.

I asked a Facebook friend who likes to post pictures of himself snuggling with his cat, who he calls his "lover," why we so often get along better with pets than with people. His answer was: "People are stupid." There are many reasons for why the love we share with animals so often seems better than what we share with each other, but it begs the question: If we got along with each other as well as we get along with our pets, would we really need pets? Our cultural notions about how love works are out of whack—stupid in their own way. Love is not nearly as heavy as we were taught it should be, as we expect it to be, or how we feel it must be.

The key is to change our perspective. Love is mysterious because we've been looking at it the wrong way. Find the right perspective, and what seemed complicated and obscure becomes simple and clear. Consider the following analogy:

The motions of the sun, moon, and planets are baffling from the perspective of the Earth, as if driven by complex, imaginary wheels within wheels—movements that mystified the ancients. Their mistake was to view it with the Earth in the center. Make the sun the center, and view the solar system from above, and the mystery melts away—its elegant simplicity emerges. In worldly things, we can control and comprehend what is simple. We cannot control and comprehend what seems unfathomably complex. The ancients got astronomy wrong because they tried to understand and explain it before the first thing about astrophysics was understood. Philosophers got love wrong because they tried to define and explain it before anything was understood about behavioral biology.

The goal of this book is to change the way we look at love, to melt away the apparently baffling complexity and obscurity, expose its elegant simplicity, then to give readers ideas they can use to help them to love better. Love is one of the greatest pleasures in life, but it is also of tremendous *practical* use. If we know how to love well, and act on that knowledge, our individual lives will be enhanced, and our collective world will be better for us all.

Changing our cultural notions of love to better match the biological nature of love is the key.

What Is Love?

Life is naturally competitive. Practically all living things are born antagonistic to each other. With few exceptions, we are, to most other living things, competitors, predators, prey, or carriers of infectious disease. Sometimes, however, we cooperate. We collect in groups of two or more to defend our territories, mates, or possessions; to gather food or to hunt prey; and to defend ourselves and each other from enemies. We presume antagonism, but crave cooperation. Love is the "switch" pulled in our brains that causes us to see another as friend instead of foe. It comes with a feeling, often a powerfully pleasant sense of affection, but understanding the function, rather than the feeling, is the key.

When you ask most anyone to tell you what they think love is, they almost always begin with "love is a feeling...", but dwelling on how love *feels* to explain how love *works* is like dwelling on how gasoline *smells* to explain how the engine makes your car go. Love is a *function*, not a feeling. Love is accompanied by a feeling. A wonderful, intense, sometimes all-encompassing feeling, but that's only its subjective manifestation. The *function* of love is to interpret another as friend instead of foe, to trust that they and you will cooperate with shared interests, and to be together with you to help, not to hurt each other.

The love/hate duality is a recurring theme of this book. Because science has learned so much about the corresponding hormones, we are better informed than all the poets and philosophers from ancient times through today.

Love, affection, trust, cooperation, kindness, and altruism are mediated to a great degree by the hormone oxytocin, sometimes called the love, or trust, hormone. Hate, fear, distrust, cruelty, and exploitation are largely mediated by stress hormones like adrenaline and cortisol. Chronic hate and fear are toxic because the stress puts aside our body's healing processes so that extra energy is momentarily available for fight or flight. Love is healing because it reduces the stress hormones, allowing the body's healing processes to fully function. We want love so we can be healthy and thrive. We don't want hate because we don't want its toxic side-effects, but life is competitive. Although we need to deal with competitors, minimizing enemies in our lives, and maximizing friends, is something worth striving for.

When we consider a person a friend, we trust they will share food, territory, possessions, companions, etc.—in other words, to be good for us.

If you love your drinking buddies, it means you trust they will welcome you, not take your drink or seat, not leave you stuck with the bar bill, not take your mate, not embarrass you, and so on. Sure, you can go out drinking with buddies you don't trust, and most likely, that feeling of affection would be missing. It's not "romantic" love, but buddy affection does share with it many of the same biological systems linked to oxytocin. This and similar hormones we share with almost all mammals. It lets us feel safe with one another. It mediates the difference between attacking or recoiling from someone versus being comfortable sitting close, feeling affectionate, touching, patting on the back, shaking hands, and the like. Again, this is not about sexual attraction. It's about trusting another's touch. It also makes eye contact safe. Ordinarily, watching another is defensive or aggressive, where we prepare to defend against attack, or to launch our own attack. Pull the brain's love switch, and eye contact becomes affectionate, not aggressive or defensive, and trust is established that hostile acts are not planned or expected.

While oxytocin is common to all mammals, similar functions, often based on similar hormones, exist in many other animals. Bees cooperate in hives. Snakes tangle together to keep each other warm. Birds gather in flocks to overwhelm predators. Even a tiny worm, the *C. elegans*, the only creature for which we now have a complete wiring diagram of their nervous system, has a pair of "RMG" nerve cells in its tiny brain that control whether or not to cuddle up to another worm of its kind. We can even go down the animal chain to

15

bacteria, some of which couple up with each other to exchange DNA—an obviously trusting moment analogous to the mating of almost all other animals, and likely working on a simple molecular mechanism to distinguish between mating friend or "eat, be eaten, or compete" enemy.

Whether it's oxytocin, or another hormone with a similar function, we are talking about a chemical code for a nonaggression pact. It switches us from "I survive alone" to "we survive together," and its manifestation in our consciousness as a feeling ranges from warm affection to overwhelming ecstasy.

The next chapter discusses the nature of feelings, and why feelings of love are so intense.

Summary of this chapter:

1—Our default relationship with nearly all living things is antagonistic: we start as either competitors, predators, or prey.

2—Love is what we typically call the feeling that accompanies a relationship that's cooperative and trustworthy and not competitive or antagonistic.

3—The most basic part of love's biology involves the "trust hormone" oxytocin. It's secreted into the brain and bloodstream as a result of certain thoughts and senses, and causes love's thoughts, urges, feelings, biological reactions, and behaviors.

What Are Feelings?

"Love is friendship set on fire."
- Jeremy Taylor [1]

Feelings are the messages from our DNA of what we should do, directly or indirectly, to spawn the next generation. In this chapter, feelings, emotions, and intuitions will be considered synonymous—to distinguish them from rationality and logic. Feelings exist because they work, or help us get along successfully in life, though often imperfectly.

A curious thing about feelings is that we use a tactile word to refer to emotions, but we tend to think of emotions as immaterial. Why do we have phrases like "Your words cut me like a knife" to express hurt feelings? Because the same brain systems that register physical injury *also* register emotional injury. Likewise, the same brain systems that register physical pleasure, especially the taste of foods we like, activate when we have emotional pleasure, which is why we have expressions like "You are sweet to say that." There is no end to metaphors that expose the strong link between emotional and physical feelings, and that is because, in some of the deepest realms of our brains, they are one and the same. It's also a big part of how we intuitively choose who we do and don't love. We are likely to have affectionate feelings toward those who touch us in pleasant ways, who smell good, or share with us food that tastes good, because the physical, and the emotional, are deeply linked.

Understanding the *reasons* for our feelings helps us control them when they aren't helpful, or when they are harmful. Love feels as important as life and death, because it is. We need love to function when we're born, to feed and to be protected, to get along in groups, and to mate and produce offspring.

The logic of feelings and emotions is unconscious, though we consciously rationalize our feelings—often incorrectly. Even our memory of past feelings is faulty. Think of all the times couples became engaged because they were certain, in their hearts, they had found the perfect partner, only to discover, at times mere minutes after the wedding ceremony, that they'd made a horrible mistake. Many then project into the past their present discomfort, and falsely believe they had an inkling of doubt that they'd ignored. Feelings, and memories of past feelings, are not always trustworthy.

Social feelings work in five steps—perception, analysis, adjustment, expression, and experience—all automatic and to a great degree, unconscious. Say, if we are approached by someone, and we pick up their facial expressions, tone of voice, scent, etc., we then analyze what we sense to decide if they are happy or unhappy, content or angry, good for us or bad for us—friend or foe. Based on this, we adjust our hormones to prepare us for how we'll handle this person: if judged friendly, we secrete oxytocin, the love and trust hormone, into our brains and bodies. If judged unfriendly, or possibly hostile, we secrete adrenaline, cortisol, and epinephrine—the fight, flight, and stress hormones. A result of hormone expression, aside from changes in how we feel, is changes in thinking and behavior. From the love and trust hormones, we are more likely to make friendly eye contact, seek skin contact, suppress stress, and feel pleasure. From the fight or flight hormones, we increase stress, defend ourselves by tensing the body and getting away from or confronting the source of stress, and we experience fearful or hostile feelings.

Feelings are not, however, the royal road to truth—to right or wrong—and don't always give us the best answers to what we should or should not do. We so often hear advice like "go with your feelings," "follow your heart," "I know in my gut what's right for me," and "my intuition is never wrong." One of your breakthroughs will be to understand their fallibility, then to learn how to handle your feelings, as well as others', for your benefit and theirs. Feelings can be manipulated, and too many of us unthinkingly follow what our feelings are telling us to do, all too often at our own peril.

The confidence we have in what the heart tells us is maintained by the psychological quirks: *confirmation bias*, which is to consider only what confirms our beliefs and ignore what doesn't; *wishful thinking*, or confusing what's true with what we want to be true; and *cognitive dissonance*, or refusal to accept evidence that our gut feelings are wrong. Someone who really believes their feelings are never wrong is vulnerable to those adept at manipulating feelings.

The phenomenon of *catfishing* (using a false identity to romance someone on the Internet) amply demonstrates the pitfalls of putting too much trust in your feelings. Countless times, an invisible suitor claimed to be a sexy model making promises of eternal love, playing on their victim's gullibility and confidence in what their hearts were telling them. It happens because of the victim's wishful thinking: confusing what they want to believe (true love) with what's real (an exploitative person who shouldn't be trusted).

Feelings are irrational, but they follow a logic all their own. Understanding their logic is key to controlling them instead of letting them control you. Feelings are interesting and useful, and should never be ignored or denied, but we must not be enslaved by them.

Animals do not ponder the meanings of their feelings. They have them, take them for granted, and let them guide their lives. We have a part of our brains above our feelings, intuitions, and instincts that helps us assess them rationally: the frontal cortex. We perceive feelings, but are not necessarily controlled by them. More precisely, we are able to postpone reward by thinking things through, and can put up with temporary hardship for future benefit in more complex ways than any other creature can. We can avoid doing things we feel like doing if we know we'll regret the consequences. Even so, it's often quite difficult. The common term for it is "discipline."

When we choose to *think* instead of behave instinctively, feelings still rise up from the primitive parts of our brains. Feelings process what's happening in the world with their own often peculiar logic, then suggest, out of impulsive desire, or from our memory banks of past experiences, what to do or not to do.

The essential categories of feelings are pleasure, what feels good, and pain, what feels bad. Pleasure tells us what our core being wants us to do, or keep doing, and pain tells us what to not do, or stop doing.

Since this book introduces new ideas, the meanings of familiar words will need to be adjusted so we don't have to coin new words. From here on, we will use slightly modified meanings of two words in particular, just to make things simpler. *Pleasure* will refer to the category of feelings that we like. Attractive sights, sounds, smells, tastes, touches, and ideas all serve to make us want to experience them more. What we want, or want more of, is suggested either by our genes or by our memories of pleasant past experiences. *Pain* will apply to what we don't like: unpleasant sights, sounds, smells, tastes, touches, and ideas we want to experience less of.

Our craving for trusting companionship with other living things is a pursuit of pleasure. Our fear of others we don't trust to be good for us is avoidance of pain. Fear, the anticipation of pain, can itself be considered painful. That is because, again, we are by default untrusting of others. A person we don't know, who's intent we are unsure of, is a person not to be trusted—to keep up our guard to. Small children instinctively hide behind their parent's legs when meeting an unfamiliar adult if not primed to trust them. However, a great deal of pleasure comes from a loving, trusting relationship, because of the benefits of cooperating rather than fighting. Once distrust is overcome, the pleasure of friendship can be intense.

The formula for engendering loving feelings—getting someone to love you—is actually quite simple. Give pleasure, and don't inflict pain. Make the person you want to love you feel good, and not feel bad. We decide if someone is friend or foe by how they make us feel. When we ask ourselves if we love someone, we ask ourselves if that person makes us feel good. If the good outweighs the bad, then there is reason to love. Want someone to love you? Always make them feel good. Never make them feel bad. They will then intuitively trust that you are good for them and won't hurt them. This kind of trust comes with those feelings, in various degrees from mild to intense, we call love.

In the next chapters, we discuss ways to make others feel good, to give them pleasure, and how to avoid making them feel bad—to not give them pain.

Summary of this chapter:

1—Feelings are what suggest to us what to do, and what not to do.

2—Feelings are fallible, often mislead us, and should not always be trusted.

3—We love people that we trust to make us feel good and not make us feel bad.

4—It's good for us to be with people we trust will make us feel good.

5—Being with people who make us feel bad is bad for us.

6—To get someone to love you, find ways to assure them they can trust you to make them feel good, and not make them feel bad.

Give Pleasure

People feel good about you if, in one way or another, they get pleasure from you—if you make *them* feel good. As obvious as this may sound, many feel that if they're loved, they needn't bother to do anything to make the ones they love feel good.

Loving is not about feeling good yourself. Make the ones you love feel good, and they will feel good about you. It can be because of something you *do*, something you do *to them*, or something about you. What you *do* that can give people pleasure can include showing a talent like singing, dancing, playing music, telling jokes, or moving gracefully. What you do *to them* could include smiling, affectionate touching, flattering, and giving food. Something *about* you could be any pleasant feature, like an attractive face, a nice body, an impressive hairdo, accessories, or clothing.

Again, some modifications of our language are needed to cover the big picture of what pleasure is about—how we give it, and how we receive it.

Whatever we want more of, what we like or makes us feel good, we will call pleasure. It can come through any of the five senses, or it can be an *idea* that triggers a pleasant feeling. The idea that someone you like wants to be with you, for example, is pleasurable without being picked up through a specific sense. Funny jokes are pleasurable, and can be read or heard. Knowing you are loved is pleasurable. Being treated to a good meal is a demonstration you are loved. Our five senses don't always have to be directly involved. That being said, here are ways our five senses pick up triggers of affection.

Sight is often considered our most important sense. This is demonstrated by how carefully many concern themselves with their appearance when looking for a mate, be it with their makeup, hair or dress, the car they drive, or the house they live in. It's usually assumed that both members of a couple should be of equal attractiveness, and an ugly guy with a pretty girl, or a handsome guy with an ugly girl, is considered peculiar. The reason we tend to fall in love with people who are physically attractive—who are eye candy—is sometimes subtle. It's partly innate, but also partly cultural and due to experiences in our upbringing. It turns out there's a natural correlation between looks and health. Good looks are a sign of health. Symmetry of facial features is usually attractive. Two differently shaped or structured eyes, for example, are considered unattractive and likely a sign of ill health. We are also sensitive to color and are likely to be judgmental about skin, eye, and hair color, usually preferring appealing colors and even tones. These are also signs of health, since skin diseases, for example, can be manifested as uneven skin coloration. Highlights on hair, however, can be attractive, because hair is a kind of plumage—the more spectacular, the more attractive, because we instinctively understand impressive plumage to also be a sign of health and well-being. How one *looks* can give us *pleasure*, and someone who gives us pleasure is more likely to be loved. Want someone to love you? Look your best.

Sound is also a primary social sense. We make judgments of each other based on our voices. A pretty, high voice in a woman, and a deep voice in a man, are usually considered attractive. An open laugh, a coo, and especially a good singing voice can also be powerful attractants. One can take voice training or read books offering advice on tuning your pipes to sound better in speech or song so you can give more pleasure with your voice.

Touch is probably the most powerful sense for triggering feelings of love. We are born wanting, indeed needing, to be in physical contact with others. It would be hard to overstate how important touch is to our well-being. Consider that love is trust, and that the first thing business people do when they meet is to shake hands, naturally promoting the trust that's essential to fruitful business deal-making. We pick up important messages in a handshake, such as whether or not he or she *wants* to touch (trust!) us, or wants to hurt us. Or, wants to assert dominance with an aggressive or threatening, hurtful grip. A cold or sweaty hand is often a sign of fear and stress, in other words, distrust or untrustworthiness. Touching is primal to the trust instinct, and therefore the love instinct. Also, how someone's skin feels can be a clue to their health. Subtleties in how one moves, when touching, can communicate affection or aggression.

Socially and romantically, one of life's wonders is the ecstasy from being touched by someone we trust completely. Our bodies have many areas set up to give us pleasure from being touched in addition to our erogenous zones. It's a statement of deep trust to allow someone to touch us in a vulnerable, delicate, or sensitive place. One of the most powerful places to receive pleasure from touch is the neck, since that is where a quick bite from an enemy can be fatal. Once trust is established and the defenses are lowered, our necks become sources of great pleasure from a loving touch, a kiss, or a nibble. It then becomes a communication of deep and confident trust and trustworthiness, and therefore, love and affection. This is a theme that repeats itself in many ways. The receiver of love says with his or her body, "I offer you my most vulnerable parts to show you how much I trust that you will not hurt me," while the lover says, "I could hurt you there, but I won't, because I am trustworthy and love you." The payoff for achieving this level of trust is intense pleasure, because our DNA has programmed us to want this. Emotional trust works the same way, using the same brain circuits as tactile trust, as if to say, "I will share with you emotionally sensitive revelations, because I trust you will not use them to hurt me." Our DNA signals to us, through these emotional mechanisms, that this is what it wants us to do—to share deep trust with another being.

Taste doesn't come into play very often in love, since it works only when we are close enough to literally receive another's molecules in our mouths. Most of our perception of taste is actually indirect perception of smell. You'll find that if you hold your nose closed and sample many foods, it becomes quite difficult and often impossible to taste them until your nose is opened again. Food becomes bland and unappealing when the nose is blocked because *most* of the taste of the food we eat is actually smelled, before it enters the mouth, while it's chewed and mixed with saliva via fumes rising up the back of the mouth, or rising up from the stomach. When we kiss, especially when we kiss deeply, we taste each other's saliva, again often indirectly via smell, which helps us detect if the person we're kissing is healthy and free of parasites, toxins, and even stress hormones. There's some perception as well of a potential mate's genetic compatibility in a kiss to the mouth or skin. It's a health check, and a person who tastes good is likely to be healthy and free of germs we could catch.

Smell—As much as we tout ourselves as visual creatures, how we smell to others, and how others smell to us, are tremendously important. The global fragrance industry, supplying good smells and eliminating bad ones to us and our environment, is estimated at forty billion US dollars annually. The way someone smells can be a live-or-die factor in the development and continuation of a relationship. Liking the way a romantic partner smells can be vital to falling in love, and staying in love.

It is phenomenal how good one's own baby smells. In fact, practically all clean and healthy babies smell great, especially to their biological parents. Imagine what taking care of infants would be like if they were born smelling bad. Babies are happily allowed to nurse, cuddle, and receive the emotional nourishment they need to survive in part because healthy newborns smell good to their mothers and fathers. A mother's nose is naturally programmed to find her offspring good in smell and taste, and a baby's biology is also programmed to give off a nice smell. Watch parents snuggling with their children, and you will likely see the mother or father plant his or her nose in the child's scalp and breath in the child's scent. That's love at the biological level, and we are only faintly aware of it much of the time. Smelling good is just one way children are set up by nature to make their parents feel good about them, and thereby encourage their love and support.

Emotions, it turns out, are about what we do to each other, and how our actions are perceived. A statement like, "You look really nice today," would be interpreted as supporting self-esteem, which is pleasurable, and the person saying it would be identified as the source of that pleasure. Through words, looks, and touch, pleasure has a secondary result of making the recipient feel good emotionally, and connecting that emotion to the person who invoked that feeling.

Our pleasure system, like most of our biology, is subject to acclimation and desensitization. That is the tendency for a repeated stimulus to, little by little, have less and less effect. Because of this, it's important both in the short term and the long term to make changes in your offerings of what your partner likes. Saying exactly the same words of love every day at the same time in the same situation in the same way has a gradually diminishing effect. It becomes robotic, and can inspire suspicions of insincerity. Change is necessary to maintain the intensity of the communications of love and affection. Changing how and where you touch, what you say, what you give, or how you look, are all helpful in maintaining someone's love for you. Otherwise, love grows stale. Changing up what you are doing to someone you love requires investment of energy and creativity, but adding variety to expressions of love is well worth the effort. Don't let repetition cause deep affection to atrophy or arouse suspicions of insincerity.

This chapter details some of the ways to make your loved ones feel good, but the variations on the theme are infinite. To love the best way you can, you need to consider how your actions or statements may affect your loved one *before* you act or speak. Ask yourself, "Will this make them feel good?" Try to picture their response. Put yourself in their shoes. When you make them feel good, make sure they know that *you* are the person making them feel good. Avoid making this too obvious, because if they feel they are being manipulated, you could lose their trust. Just don't let it be missed that you are responsible for their good feelings.

As important to making the ones you love feel good is to avoid making them feel bad—the subject of the next chapter.

Summary of this chapter:

1—What you are and what you do can make people feel good.

2—You'll be loved by people who trust you will make them feel good.

3—What you are that gives people pleasure is picked up by their senses—how you look, sound, taste, smell, and touch.

4—What you do can make people feel good about you, like demonstrating talent, support, or affection.

5—Try not to be repetitive in what you do to make your partner feel good, since repetition can result in acclimation and desensitization. The effect gets lesser and lesser, and may even seem insincere and mechanical rather than honestly affectionate.

Don't Inflict Pain

"You Always Hurt the One You Love"
-Allan Roberts[2]

Like the song says, we certainly do, too often, hurt the ones we love, and certainly shouldn't.

Tony's former girlfriend had two lovely children from her previous marriage, an eight-year-old girl and a five-year-old boy, and the four of them enjoyed their time together. One evening on a walk, the boy reached for and held Tony's hand, and smiled warmly to him. Tony smiled back. Then the boy clamped down on Tony's hand as hard as he could, causing quite a bit of pain, which Tony endured to avoid spoiling the tender moment. After a minute of this, the boy cheerfully told Tony that he liked him because, unlike his father, he didn't complain when he hurt him. Tony could have felt smug about having a leg up as a prospective stepfather, but the boy was, unfortunately, on track to squander present and

33

future affection. It's likely his father lost some of his son's affection by complaining angrily about being held too tightly, starting a back-and-forth cycle of emotional injury.

The notorious line from Erich Segal's novel and film, *Love Story*, about love meaning never having to say you're sorry, is often misinterpreted and therefore misquoted as, "love means never saying you're sorry." The deeper meaning in the phrase is almost always missed. It doesn't have to mean never telling the ones you love you are sorry. It could mean you should not do things to your partner that you will need to apologize for. In other words, don't inflict pain, or, don't make the ones you love feel bad. If mutual love is alive, you and your partner will trust each other and understand that neither of you will intentionally cause the other's suffering, and therefore, will not cause intentional or negligent harm you will need to apologize for. This is a simple rule to not spoil the love someone has, or could have, for you. Just don't hurt them.

Like pleasure, pain also comes to us from the five senses and the emotions.

Fear is the feeling that warns us that we might be harmed in some way. It's our internal alarm. One of the most primitive fears that keeps people apart, that blocks intimacy and affection, is fear of disease. It's not always a conscious, rational fear. It's a distaste or disgust that protects us from parasitic, bacterial, or viral infections—you know, germs. It involves fear of looks, smells, even sounds like a cough or hoarse voice, that some argue are shallow and superficial, but are actually manifestations of instinctive defenses. Our perception of what we find revolting is, however, imperfect. Many things smell terrible but are not bad for us at all. By and large, for our ancestors, finding some things revolting helped keep them safe from parasites and infections. We can get used to things that are revolting, and we can be repelled by things that are harmless. Kids say a person they find repellant has "cooties" they don't want to catch, and this is a hint of our instinctive fear of parasites and infections. We just need to learn to accept and understand the imperfections of this natural defense mechanism. Most of the time, we are a bit better off with such mechanisms, like fear of "cooties," than we would be without them.

There is a compensating mechanism: acclimation, or, getting used to an unattractive feature. It's what's behind the idea of knowing the person inside, or not being "shallow." It can be about overcoming a bad first impression and getting to know more deeply someone you initially found unattractive. It can apply to someone you grew up with who always had some unattractive physical feature. Or, you might be able to ignore an unattractive feature in someone you already knew well *before* the feature developed.

Smell is a sense well-tuned to warn us of danger—usually the danger of infectious disease. Fans of *Seinfeld* may remember the episode where Kramer wore bad-smelling things to remove his "kavorka" (animal sexual attraction) to cure a nun of her crush on him.

There are actually no good smells or bad smells. We interpret some smells as bad if they typically come from something infectious or toxic we needed to avoid. Think of how unlikely you will want to be friends with someone you just met who smells awful. They don't even need to smell bad, themselves, since all we need to do is associate a bad smell with the person. For example, meet a person at a party for the first time when at the same moment foul-smelling cheese fumes waft into our nostrils from the buffet table, and we are challenged to like the person if we then associate the person with the smell. This is, of course, an irrational association, since the person is not producing the odor, but the machinery of our emotions, instincts, and intuitions is faulty and does its own thing in its own way. It doesn't think, but responds in preprogrammed ways by connecting things found together. Deep in our brains, a courting target can be associated with a repellent cheese smell. It's a challenge to overcome this when it happens. Conscious knowledge of the real source of the smell is not likely to be sufficient, because the association has gotten under the skin to become a gut reaction disconnected from our flexible, intelligent thoughts. Accidents happen. Interestingly, the gut reaction to someone we associate with a bad smell is a natural defense against anticipated ingestion of toxins, and it literally does happen in the gut. In other words, the reaction to something disgusting is your digestive system arming itself against a chemical or biological threat. The "gut" is even at times called by neurobiologists our "second brain" because it has some 100 million neurons—about the same number as a mouse's brain.

The message here is that if you want people to be attracted to you, don't smell bad, and don't hang around bad smells people could unconsciously attribute to you. This is easier said than done. We often cannot smell ourselves because we are used to our own smells. Follow good hygiene, of course, don't be careless about passing gas or eating smelly foods around people whose affections you desire, and don't court in smelly places. The target of your interest may connect the smell to you, and their instinctive defenses against contagious germs may doom their interest.

Additionally, people's body odors communicate things other than disease. We almost literally smell fear on a person under stress because we actually smell the breakdown products of their stress hormones in their sweat. It's an unpleasant smell because our instincts understand that people under stress might be dangerous. For example, our instincts could be telling us that the person that we perceive through our sense of smell to be under stress may actually be pretending to be our friend, but secretly intend to betray us. It's useful to smell this. Our instincts tell us that someone who is calm is probably safe and may even like us. Otherwise, if you can smell their stress, then watch out!

Touch is one of the most important senses in affection. We love to be touched by people we trust, and shrink away from contact with those we distrust—not just painful contact, but from just about any kind of physical contact.

One important thing to avoid is premature contact—touching someone who doesn't quite trust you yet. It's likely to make his or her skin "crawl," an appropriate metaphor we use because it triggers the same instinctive revulsion we feel when an insect or small animal is crawling on us. It's an important instinct because a bite from such a creature is likely to poison us or to give us some kind of disease—even lay a parasitic egg that will hatch later and make us dangerously ill. The repurposing of this instinct that protects us from creepy, crawling insects, to protecting us from unsure social contact, is exactly the kind of thing we would expect nature to do.

An important thing to be careful of is to keep your loving touch feeling good. When you are giving love through touch (hugging, caressing, or stroking), don't get too lost in how it feels to *you*. Keep your attention on how it feels to *them*. Don't hug so tightly you cause pain. Don't hold longer than your partner wants to be held. Don't stroke repeatedly in the same spot until it starts to chafe. Don't press too hard or for too long. Don't touch a sensitive area that is injured or healing. Your partner wants reassurance, deep down, consciously and unconsciously, that you will not hurt them. It's not that difficult to avoid hurting people because we purportedly have in our brains "mirror neurons" that help us feel what someone else feels, almost as if we were feeling it ourselves. Both instinctively and through learned experience, we *know* how to touch people in ways unlikely to cause discomfort or pain. We just have to take advantage of this inborn skill to feel what others feel if we want to be loved and not hurt the ones we love.

Sight is another sense we use to pick up information about each other that is especially useful because it works at a distance. A cosmetics advertisement on TV, with the theme "accuracy matters," shows a pretty woman putting on makeup in a mirror, her face out of our view. She then turns to the camera and smiles, showing she'd accidentally put red lipstick on one of her front teeth. Suddenly, in our primitive gut response, she's repulsive, and the message our deeper brain receives is that she's ill and we should keep our distance, or we might catch whatever she's got that's rotted her tooth. There's also a movie scene I recall where a couple is on a first date at a restaurant. The superbly handsome and eligible guy is making great conversation, and everything is going well until he smiles broadly, revealing a piece of spinach from the salad stuck to a front tooth. It ended the date. Obviously, we know consciously that a bit of spinach can be cleaned from one's tooth in a flash, no big deal, and that it's no indication of disease. Our revulsion, however, is an automatic gut reaction, and the gut does not understand sophisticated modern inventions like toothpicks, brushes, or mouthwash.

Even though some of these examples are from fiction (movies and TV), they play on real human reactions audiences understand. They are not always rational. Teeth can be quickly cleaned to restore their pearly glory. What *can* happen though, especially if a disturbing sight was part of a first impression, is that the image can return to our minds at critical later moments of intimacy.

We want to look at things that look pleasant and avoid looking at things that look bad. It's unfortunate that trivial details of appearance can harm our mission of finding love, but the way love works is imperfect. When unpleasant images come back to us while we are trying to close the deal, fulfilling our need to be loved is challenged. What we have is a kind of early warning system to protect us from things we "don't like the looks of" that, while not necessarily painful to look at, are nevertheless on our innate or learned lists of things we don't like—a warning to keep our distance.

Sound can also be repellent, and can also be an early warning of disease. The sound of passing gas at either end is a notorious turn-off on a first date, because we know it's likely to come with a bad smell, which, again, would be warning of contagious disease.

Voices matter, too. There's a famous episode of *Seinfeld* where a girl, apparently perfect in every way, had a horrific laugh that killed off any possibility of Jerry wanting intimacy with her. A hoarse or gravelly voice or cough can telegraph a contagious throat infection. It's not easy to date someone with an unpleasant voice, and it's likely to be a deal-killer in a courtship.

Taste, like smell, also helps us detect disease in a mate. In courtship, a kiss is likely the final check before acceptance that a prospective mate is disease-free, since it's an exchange of fluids after the other filters of sight, sound, touch, and smell have done their jobs. We also actually taste and smell each other's DNA, indirectly, via sensing certain proteins, and tend to find that genetically unsuitable mates taste unpleasant in a kiss.

Emotional pain comes from ideas sensed from situations that come in through our five senses. We could be hurt by a facial expression, unkind words spoken or written, another's physical violence, their recoil from affection, or betrayal.

Like the chapter on giving pleasure, this chapter attempts to detail typical ways you should avoid making your loved ones feel bad, but the variations are infinite. To love the best way you can, you need to consider how your actions or statements will affect your loved ones before you act. Ask yourself, "will this make them feel bad?" Try to picture their response. View things from their perspective. Based on what you know about them, or how you'd react yourself, consider how your planned action will make them feel. If you hurt them in some way by accident, make sure your loved ones know it was not your intention, and make sure they are convinced of your regret. Whoever it is, your mother, father, sister, brother, child, lover, or pet, try to never give them pain or hurt them if you love them. Never be identified by them as a source of their pain.

The next chapter goes more deeply into the sense of smell and its often-neglected but crucial role in human relations.

Summary of this chapter:

1—Hurting someone, disgusting them, or otherwise making them feel bad can prevent them from loving you, or make them stop loving you.

2—Keep up good hygiene so you don't smell bad and disgust the people you want to love you.

3—Be conscious of how you are perceived. Don't look or sound repulsive. Don't touch in ways that hurt. Don't make bad smells, or be around bad smells someone you want to love you could associate with you.

4—Don't carelessly hurt your loved one's feelings.

The Nose Knows the Chemistry of Love

We don't smell everything our noses detect. When we say we have good chemistry with a person we love, it can literally mean that passionate feelings have been triggered via chemicals passed from the person to their lover's nose *unaccompanied by any conscious smell.*

The nose's olfactory bulb is directly connected to the emotional center of the brain—the amygdala. That is why, when we smell something from our past, we may experience an intense moment of emotional memory. Some smells are passed on to the rest of the brain to our consciousness, but others aren't, even when they trigger strong emotional or hormonal responses. It's just the way we are wired, and understanding a bit about our wiring can help us understand the nature of love, to help us take charge of our love life, and not let it take charge of us.

Many emotions produce hormones in our bloodstream that relay information around the body—but these hormones, or their breakdown products, find themselves in our sweat glands, salivary glands, and mucus membranes, where they evaporate into the air and then communicate information to others. When they do this we call them pheromones. This principle is manifested in our language in phrases like, "I smell a rat," which hints at how perceptions about people are intuitively picked up by our noses. "My lover and I have good chemistry" is more than a metaphor. It's a hint of what's really happening in us, biologically.

One of the inspirations for this book (mentioned in the introduction) was a moment in Dr. Robert Sapolsky's Stanford lecture series on behavioral biology (#15: Human Sexual Behavior). He pointed out the irony that women tended to buy and apply perfumes that *they* found attractive, not what *men* thought were sexy. This provoked the strategic question from a male student along the lines of, "would I smell attractive to women if I wore a perfume women liked to put on themselves?" (The student's exact words are not known because his voice was unintelligible in the video). Strategic ideas like his, based on biological knowledge, are a key theme of this book.

Some essential ingredients in perfumes and colognes are not accompanied by smells we are conscious of, but can still produce intense emotional responses. Fertile men like the smell of fertile women, and fertile women like the smell of fertile men, and these differing smells are, to a great degree, subconscious. In other words, we could mix a male's pheromone with the smell of General Tso's Chicken, and to a woman it may smell like any other

44

General Tso's Chicken but she'd find herself inexplicably wanting to jump under the sheets with the nearest handsome guy. Likewise, female pheromones blended with licorice jelly beans could make a man feel ready for action while thinking he's smelling ordinary dollar store candy.

So, a woman who wants to smell sexy is likely to use a product like Chanel® No 5, because she and her female shopping partners find it sexy. Its original secret ingredient, it turns out, was the sweat of whipped Abyssinian cats—*male* cats (now synthesized so cats no longer need to be tortured for the pleasure of millions of female shoppers). When women apply it, they make themselves smell like a fertile male, not a female, which women like, but men don't. To women, the response to sniffing it is, "ooh, that's sexy." Men's response to the same smell is to feel aggression against a competitor, or, "Fee-fi-fo-fum I smell the blood of an Englishman." Unconscious, for sure, yet it explains why men are often disdainful of women's perfumes, and women are unimpressed by perfumes men ask them to wear. A strategic suggestion to women who want to smell sexy to men is to wear perfumes men, not women, find sexy. Likewise, a man who wants to attract women by applying a scent might be smart to choose a product marketed to women.

The other way smells affect romantic attraction has to do with immunocompatibility. We literally like the smell of someone who has the disease-fighting genes we lack, so we can add them to our genome in the hope of producing children who will be able to fight both the diseases we and our partner are innately good at fighting. This principle, that we are attracted to mates who have features we like but don't have in ourselves, is commonly misinterpreted as "opposites attract," and extends to other features, like hair and eye color, body type, interests, talents, and so forth.

The next chapter expands on touch, the other sense too often neglected for its vital role in the human connection.

Summary of this chapter:

1—What we smell, consciously and unconsciously, directly affects the emotional part of our brains.

2—Emotions have smells, and the smell of emotions comes from the breakdown products of the hormones associated with those emotions emitted in body sweat and, likely, other bodily fluids.

3—A smell attractive to us may be unattractive to those we want to attract.

4—We smell, indirectly, each other's DNA, and tend to be sexually attracted to those whose DNA is a bit different from our own.

The Loving Touch

"I found that of all the senses the eye was the most superficial, the ear the most haughty, smell the most voluptuous, taste the most superstitious and inconstant, touch the most profound and philosophical."
- Diderot [3]

Every night, Barbara and Arthur, after switching off the light, held each other in their arms, as closely as they could, entangling their legs and enjoying the ecstasy of touching every inch of skin together. Extreme skin contact is love's payoff—the friendship on fire. The next day, Arthur was to use his inheritance check to make a down payment on their first house, but instead lost all the money trying to run it up beforehand at the racetrack. When he revealed to Barbara the money was gone, a terrible fight ensued. After the lights went out, Arthur moved to Barbara's side of the bed and embraced her with his arms and legs exactly as he had the night before, and every night before that since they'd been together. Barbara shuddered. She turned coldly to him and said it was like being in the clutches of an octopus trying to crush her. "This is how it feels," she added, and held him exactly the same way *she* always had before, and he felt the crushing octopus wrapping its deadly tentacles around him. The formerly ecstatic embrace of love became a hateful death grip. Though *physically the same*—each arm and leg did nothing different from the night before—the same exact act, something wonderful became something horrible because trust was gone. To enjoy physical embrace is to enjoy trust.

The *loving touch* is physical contact with someone you trust won't hurt you. Allowing the touch indicates acceptance of trustworthiness. While there can be individual variation in how much touch is too little or too much—we each may have a different sweet spot—we tend to want to touch people we trust, and want to be touched by them. We avoid touching people we distrust, and recoil from their attempts to establish trust with unwelcome contact. You can think of it as a litmus test of friendship. Watch who people touch, and their reactions to being touched, and you know instantly if they are, deep down inside, friend or foe (given that they're not faking it).

Along with smell, touch is a sense profoundly linked to all types of love. Our bodies need the squirts of oxytocin hormone regularly to stay healthy. We are born to be touched by the family that spawned us, and grow up to touch and be touched by the family we create. We seek touch from each other in small ways, like handshakes and

48

pats on the back, and in larger ways, like hugs and pecks on the cheeks. In many sports, a pat on the rear is an expected congratulation.

Affectionate touching comes in a number of levels. There's simple contact like touching someone briefly on the shoulder, shaking the hand, and air kissing. Then, there's grooming, tickling, and so on in continuation all the way to sexual contact. Acceptance of another's touch communicates acceptance of affection. Rejecting touch signals a failed connection, as if to say, "I am not your friend," or, "I *don't trust* you."

Grooming is a step up from simple affectionate touch. Although common in close relationships, we spontaneously also develop affections for hairdressers, doctors, masseurs, chiropractors, manicurists, and pedicurists, because those professions involve tactile grooming we instinctively interpret as affectionate, independent of their professional formality.

Next up is tickling. The signal you give when you tickle someone properly is, "I want to make you feel good." Children love to be tickled by people they like. They indeed sometimes *demand* it. We tend to enjoy ticking less and less as we grow older, because, while as children we are likely to be around family and friends we trust, growing up brings us into contact with ever more individuals we mustn't trust. Being tickled by someone we dislike is torture while the same precise tickling motion can be delightful from trusted family or close friends.

Then, there's humor. Ever wonder why we laugh when we're tickled, and also laugh when we are entertained by something funny? It's because humor tickles the brain. We'd laugh hysterically at a joke told by someone we liked, but refuse to laugh if the same joke were told by someone we didn't. We want to joke with our friends and don't want to humor our enemies. One exception, consistent with this thesis, is using humor to defuse enemies and convert them to friends. Comedians often report they used this tactic when explaining how they got started in comedy (to disarm bullies).

The connection between emotions and tactile sensations runs deep. The language of love is riddled with metaphors of physical touch, for a good biological reason. The hormones and regions of the brain stimulated by physical touch are also stimulated in emotional responses to situations. Its why emotions are called feelings, and why we ask if we are in *touch* with our feelings. We say a kind word touches us deeply while a cruel word is like a knife through the heart. An affectionate person is warm-hearted, and a cold shoulder refers to social rejection. We panic when someone we love touches us with cold fingers, because we instinctively know withdrawal of blood from extremities accompanies stress. These are *not* just poetic analogies. They are manifestations of the natural wiring of the brain.

Members of many cultures, particularly those that fear intimacy, are starving for physical contact with one another. Sometimes called *skin hunger* (Floyd), they live in a state of tragic tactile loneliness, and therefore find countless alternate though less effective ways to get the touching they need. They get pets they can stroke. They go for massages and chiropractic manipulations. They smoke, an echo of the suckling of infancy. They hold pillows and stuffed animals. They sit in vibrating massage chairs or switch on magic finger beds. They find excuses to touch in square dancing and sports. All are ways to find some way to be touched safe from the restrictions of their culture's prohibitions and taboos.

Now we have phone, text, Skype, and other online relationships. Curiously, they can be among the most intense. Cyberspace's deprivation of tactile communication sets one up for incomparable heights of angst-filled romance. This intensity is a result of the gap between what we are getting (touchless romance) and what we need (physical skin contact).

Let's revisit warmth while we're talking about the loving touch. I had a girlfriend as a teen who, if my hands were cold for any reason, couldn't resist repeating the cliche, "cold hands, warm heart." It's likely she was doing this to quiet her instinct to interpret cold hands as unloving, as if afraid to lose confidence in the emotional connection. Warmth is important to us as well as to all animals, perhaps especially to us warm-blooded ones. We equate, intuitively, body warmth with closeness and affection. Being cold is like being alone. When we're cold, we naturally want to receive warmth from someone we trust. Two held together against the cold is also a metaphor for uniting to feel safe against a hostile world, and that's, well, the very definition of love.

Pleasure, pain, feeling good, and feeling bad are all transformed into emotions associated with hormones, the body's messengers. A novel way to think about hormones is the theme of our next chapter.

Summary of this chapter:

1—We are wired to need and enjoy touching people we trust.

2—Affectionate touch releases in our bodies the love and trust hormone, oxytocin.

3—We accept touch from people we trust and recoil from people we don't.

4—Grooming and tickling are important types of affectionate touch, and humor, which can be thought of as tickling the brain, likewise communicates friendship and affection.

5—Too many people live in cultures or situations deprived of the essential, instinctively necessary physical contact with people they trust.

6—The affectionate touch is at the very heart of what love is.

The Language of Hormones

"Love is indeed, at root, the product of the firings of neurons and release of hormones."
- Julian Baggini [4]

Dr. Baggini made the statement as an example of how science may answer the "how" of love in biochemical terms, but not the "why." That being said, there's a great deal we can learn about what love is, how love works, and how to love better by understanding the language of its hormones.

When people mention hormones, it's usually in the context of hitting puberty—lowering the voice and growing body hair and beards in boys, growing breasts and shapely form in girls, and developing attractions to the opposite sex. However, hormones are involved in many other functions of human and animal bodies in addition to sexual maturity. More than 800 hormones are currently known to be functioning in the human body.

A hormone is a message. A growth hormone sends the message from the body's biological clock, also following nutritional and social cues, to inform various parts of the body to grow. Hormones of sexual maturity are messages also from the internal clock and nutritional and social cues, to cause maturation of sexual features in the bodies and brains of boys and girls to become men and women, produce eggs and sperm, change looks, physique, attitudes, interests, and so on, and so forth. In the language of hormones, they are saying "time to make little ones."

Before we go further, it's worth noting that the science facts in this book are of the current prevailing understanding of biology, behavior, and hormones. Some studies are pending replication, update, or are in dispute, but that's the nature of science—continuously improving our understanding of the world, ourselves, and each other via steady, incremental corrections and refinements of our body of knowledge.

A hormone message is a chemical—a molecule made up of two or more atoms. Communication with hormones means one part of the body produces a specific hormone, the message, and another part receives it. In one conversation I had about the hormone of love and trust, oxytocin, someone pondered what, exactly, it was about the molecule that had to do with love. It couldn't be the two sulfur atoms embracing each other in a cosy azanide-guarded love nest, could it? I'm joking. The answer is: *nothing at all!* There is nothing intrinsically loving about the hormone oxytocin. Any molecule would do, just like there's nothing special about the word *love*. Any other word would do, as long as it's said by someone intending to discuss love, and heard by someone who knows what the word's about. The actual word has no intrinsic meaning except to the person saying it and the person hearing it. Likewise, there's nothing loving about the molecule oxytocin, except that it's produced in the body when functions related to love are needed, and received in parts of the body that in one way or another, directly or indirectly, carry out its functions. Oxytocin is a word in the body's language of hormones, and the best translation of that molecule's meaning to English is *trust*.

Most, if not all emotions, are associated with hormones, although most hormones swirl about in our bloodstreams and body fluids without any direct conscious feeling of their presence or absence. When we feel a particular emotion, our bodies produce a particular hormone. It turns out, also, that when our bodies or brains are medically injected with an emotion hormone, we'll experience or act on that emotion.

To understand emotions, so often thought to be subjective, personal, and unfathomable, we need to list the events that cause the body to make emotion hormones, the parts of the body that receive hormonal messages, and the actions that result from their presence. Some additional factors that inform us of the workings of emotion hormones include: what inhibits their production or reception, how quickly a hormone level rises when it's produced, and how quickly it falls off after production stops.

This is not just technical stuff useless in the real world of our daily lives. It is profoundly informative and pragmatically useful.

Let's start with oxytocin.

Hugging someone you affectionately trust causes your oxytocin level to rise. It's been found, however, that it takes about 20 seconds for the rise to be really significant (Grewen, et al., U. of North Carolina). This is one reason why a hug that's too brief is considered insincere. We don't "feel" it. We might therefore conclude that, to give a hug that will be perceived as sincere, one would make sure the hug lasts at least 20 seconds. I've even suggested to a filmmaker friend that if he wants the audience to feel the affection of an onscreen hug or caress, he should keep its length to at least 20 seconds (480 film frames, or 30 feet of movie film). Yes, science usefully contributes to the arts! Oxytocin, however, doesn't linger long in the brain or bloodstream. Its half-life, when the effects begin to significantly wear off after a hug ends because its molecules are breaking down, is about 1-4 minutes at body temperature. You can think of this as an emotion that needs a periodic recharge in the form of more hugs, touches, eye contact, kind words, and so forth to keep doing its job. The breakdown can also be interpreted as a defense mechanism to return us to our normal state of trust versus distrust, appropriately timed. It would be quite dangerous to remain in a generally trusting state for hours after a goodbye hug from your spouse before encountering rush hour traffic and a day at a competitive workplace.

The thoughts and actions that cause oxytocin release are fascinating. They include pregnancy, signals in the environment of safety, friendly eye or skin contact, body warmth, grooming, laughter, stretching of the birth canal (for women), looking at breasts (for men), sexual arousal, and orgasm. Oxytocin is blocked by stress, threats, an unfamiliar environment, lack of privacy, and perception of insincere affection. Oxytocin's effects include social bonding, trust, generosity, concern for others, reduced fear and aggression and blood pressure, onset of labor, and production of breast milk. It's also been found that administering oxytocin artificially can cure postpartum depression. It's even been found to suppress boredom, presumably to allow people who like or love each other to enjoy each other's company without having to be distracted and entertained. It's been discovered that gossiping—disparaging an absent individual—raises oxytocin levels (Brondino, Fusar-Poli, Politi), as if to say, "I trust you because we have a common enemy." We cover this at length in the chapter, "I Love You Because You Hate Who I Hate." Such is the sprawling nature of our body's message of trust. Because of this hormone's multipurpose functions for both friendly affection and sexual arousal, some crosstalk can occur that makes for confusion and poor social choices, especially when it causes development of inappropriate sexual interest in close friendship or business relationships (more on this in the final chapter, "Why Isn't There More Love in the World?").

So, in the language of the hormone oxytocin, what causes it to flow are reasons to trust someone. Its flow is inhibited by signs we should be distrustful, and its actions are about how our behaviors differ towards those we trust versus those we do not trust.

A hormone related to oxytocin in form and function is vasopressin. In the body, it regulates hydration, but inside the brain, separated from the body by the blood-brain barrier, it enables a neural pathway between the special person we love deeply and our reward and pleasure centers. In the body, the vasopressin message is, "hold on to water," but in the brain, it says something along the lines of, "feel good about, desire, and hold on to this person, forsaking all others." It's the monogamy hormone.

The messages of hormones, however, are not always limited to the domain of a single person's body. Some hormones, and their breakdown products, are secreted in sweat, saliva, and tears, for others to smell and taste. In this way, the messages in hormones are communicated not just within our bodies, but from person-to-person, and often unconsciously. Then we call them pheromones. We can smell fear, and we need to for good biological reasons. The sweat of a tense, stressed-out person is distinctive. Can we smell love? More research is needed. That the dog's sense of smell is thousands of times better than ours is one reason why they have such remarkable emotional connections with their owners, and seem to sense the trustworthiness of strangers. When I meet a golden retriever, a breed of dogs who are angels to me, it almost seems like she smells the cartoon hearts circling my head, and in short order is all over me pawing, pressing against me and licking enthusiastically.

One extraordinary example of hormones as languages of interpersonal communication is crying. Why do we cry? Because we are sad? What, then, are tears of joy? The composition of tears contains the answer. They include the breakdown products of stress hormones. Inside you, stress hormones arm you for conflict and struggle, like dealing with enemies or coping with loss and hardship. When they are no longer needed, when the hardship is over, the stress hormones need to be removed. They are unhealthy to keep around. A mechanism we have to dispense with stress hormones is in the tear glands of our eyes. We literally cry away stress, and additionally, the act of crying tells others we no longer want to struggle. Tears of sadness are to remove excess stress to accept loss. Tears of joy are to transition you from coping with what you are missing, like a treasured friend or relative, to enjoying their return. It takes you from having to harden your heart when someone you love is away or in danger, to softening your heart on their return or when you learn they are safe. The cancellation of stress through crying is also a message to others that we are de-stressing. We should stop telling people not to cry. Painful as it sometimes is, crying is good for you if with people who are safe to show your tears.

There are a number of reasons why we'd move from fight-or-flight to safety, and corresponding reasons why we'd be discouraged from crying. We might be told not to cry in an attempt to comfort us after disappointment, but crying is necessary for recovery, and should be encouraged, not discouraged. Crying is also a signal that we don't want to fight, but this can be seen as a sign of weakness. Bullies understand this instinctively, which is why they see a potential victim who is prone to cry as vulnerable to cruel treatment. A crying victim is one who will not fight back. Crying telegraphs vulnerability to an enemy, but it's vital in a loving relationship for it to be safe to cry.

Understanding the functions, causes, and effects of hormones helps us understand ourselves, and each other. Our biology, and how it interacts with the environment, determines who we are and what we do. From that understanding comes empathy and forgiveness for behaviors that, unfortunately in some cultures, inspire contempt. While not necessarily excusing bad behavior, the contempt some cultures hold for what's natural poisons our trust and affection for each other and isolates us to our great personal and collective peril. While we need not be slaves of our hormonal impulses, we can choose to stop condemning each other and ourselves for the impulses and urges the admittedly uneven wisdom of the ages has imprinted on us.

The next chapter fills in the discussion of trust in greater detail, and its vital importance in the story of love.

Summary of this chapter:

1—Hormones are messengers within the body, from one body part to another.

2—Pheromones can be thought of as hormones that communicate between one person and another.

3—While oxytocin is, in a very general way, the hormone of affection and trust, vasopressin, when excreted locally in the brain, has a particular role in attaching a specific mate to feelings of intense pleasure, especially deep romantic love.

4—What causes emotional hormones to be excreted into the brain and body, and what changes they produce, usefully informs us about how our emotions actually work and how we may cope with them.

Trust

"He who does not trust enough will not be trusted."
-Lao Tzu [5]

An ad for a local HVAC/plumbing repair business shows a woman sing-speaking, "I love those guys," the subtext being that, since she trusts her repair technicians, you should too. The advertisers understand the equivalency of love and trust, since it's almost impossible to love someone you don't trust, and sincere demonstrations of trust are demonstrations of love.

As a human experience, love and trust are inseparable because of love's biological foundation. Many statements about either can survive a simple word substitution and hardly change. "I trust him, but I'm afraid he doesn't trust me" reads about the same as "I love him, but I'm afraid he doesn't love me." This principle, the equivalency of love and trust, covers all the different kinds of love, romantic and otherwise. "I love my doctor" actually means you *trust* your doctor. "I love my boss, neighbors, teammates, etc." also means you trust them. To lose trust in someone you love is to stop loving them. You may love who the person was, as a memory of someone you once trusted in the past, but not the untrustworthy person in the present (this is the "different person" model we discuss in the later chapter "Restoring Lost Love").

But what if, say, you love your cousin, but don't trust your cousin to drive your car? We're talking about trusting someone as a whole—trusting that he or she will not want to harm you, physically, financially, or emotionally. They will not intend to make you feel bad, and is a friend, not an enemy.

Intent to be trustworthy, however, is not magical. Someone you love can *intend* to be good for you, but repeated failure to be trustworthy can be fatal to love. Someone who doesn't groom well enough to look or smell good, or to not organize themselves well enough to follow through on promises, will damage feelings of love you may have for them. It's possible that such lack of consideration is a subtle form of hostility, in the form of passive aggression, but it can also simply be from innocent bad habits of social conduct. To be loved means to be trusted to be good for the person who loves you. To annoy or harm the person who loves you is understandably interpreted as unloving, regardless of intent. Love is often taken for granted, as in Western culture's assumption that love is forever, but the truth is that repeated minor breaches of trust, or even a single major breach, can be fatal to a loving relationship.

The foundation of the Baywatch TV show's erotic appeal isn't just in the sexy stars in revealing swimsuits, but in the trust we take for granted from a lifeguard. They exist to rescue us. Lifeguards are presumed to be trustworthy people. Likewise are fireman, first aid responders, doctors, and nurses. Their function is to help you, and given no evidence to the contrary, they tend to be desirable, simply because trust is understood to be built into their job descriptions.

Then, there's paranoia, which can be thought of as a pathological collapse of trust. At clinical levels, paranoia becomes an impenetrable certainty that no one is trustworthy—that everyone, regardless of their conduct and appearance, is an enemy. The sufferer believes no one loves them. Stress hormones become locked in and oxytocin is locked out. It even becomes a vicious circle where attempts to reestablish trust are interpreted as insincere and are met with even deeper distrust—a cycle that may be impossible to break. The only chance one has to help someone stricken with paranoidal distrust is through persistent reassurance and repeated demonstrations of trustworthiness.

Animals demonstrate real loving trust. Ever notice how cats close their eyes to someone they love? It's because cats are usually loners and normally hostile to one another. They watch each other so they are ready to defend themselves against attack, making closing their eyes a powerful statement of trust. Cats stare hard at those they dislike, and close their eyes to those they like, as if to say: "I will let you know that I completely trust you won't hurt me. I do not need to watch you to feel safe." Intimacy can escalate to offers of grooming, licking each other, and offering the parts of their bodies most vulnerable to injury like the belly—the ultimate position of defenselessness—as further statements of trust. The deal is completed when they fall asleep together, because one can't possibly be more vulnerable than when one is unconscious. The internal manifestation of such demonstrations of complete trust is the intense pleasure of love—the "friendship on fire."

Complete trust is good for us, because two beings working together are better off by far than working apart, or against each other, and we instinctively understand this. It's coded in our DNA. There is ecstasy to be found in trust.

Summary of this chapter:

1—Trust is at the very heart of interpersonal love.

2—Someone can fully intend to be trustworthy but fail. Intent is not magical.

3—There is ecstasy to be found in a deep trusting relationship because we know, instinctively, how valuable it is.

Why We Need Love

Thirteenth century King Frederick II of Sicily wanted to know what language children spoke (Latin, it was suspected) if raised from birth with almost no human contact, so he commandeered a number of babies to be raised with every necessity and ordinary comfort, but no touching, affection, or human connection. They all died in infancy.

There are four things we need that are essential to life: air, water, food, and companionship, listed here in order of how quickly their absence will kill us. Without air we are likely to die of hypoxia in about three minutes. Without water, we'll expire from dehydration in three days or so. Lifetime expectancy without food is three weeks. Individual cases vary. These are averages. Social isolation also threatens survival. The mortality risk from loneliness has been found to be comparable to smoking and obesity. It raises risks of arthritis, type II diabetes, and heart disease. Loneliness doubles the risk of premature death for the elderly. We have many ways to keep social starvation from killing us quickly, but it's tendency to make our lives unpleasant, short and unhealthful is a near certainty.

We are social creatures. Our natural state is to be with others of our kind, like family, friends, and coworkers. But some of us are alone or living in toxic social groups. We may live with toxic parents, siblings, neighbors, or coworkers. Many are isolated because they've been hurt in the past by family or associates, and we'd often rather be around people we don't like or trust than to be alone. We are seldom, however, completely alone. We compensate for loneliness with online social networks, vicarious socialization from movies or television or reading, enjoying the company of pets, or fantasizing, rehearsing, or recalling social interactions in our heads.

Perhaps the worst a person can be made to suffer for violating mores is social isolation. Shunning is an ultimate punishment in many cultures. Social rejection can cause major psychological damage and is sometimes thought of as torture, even something as apparently mild as making children sit alone in a corner while watching other children play together. Many prisoners who've endured prolonged solitary confinement suffer permanent psychological damage.

We are born wired to understand that we are safer in groups than by ourselves, so being alone is likely to cause stress hormones to flow through our bodies that suppress normal operation of our immune systems, making us vulnerable to infections. Stress suppresses healing and cell and organ maintenance and upsets the normal progress of inflammations, which can then directly damage our organs. Loneliness can even trigger depression and antisocial behaviors that push people away, initiating a downward spiral of social failure.

Teamwork is powerful. In a hostile world, you stand a better chance to survive and do well if you're not alone. The world is less fearful. You have each others' backs. Best of all, you see each other as friends and not enemies, so you can let your guard down and dispense with the toxic hormones of fear. Your body can step up the processes of healing and fighting infections. It will be safe to relax and heal rather than be on guard and defend yourself against injury, physical or emotional. You'll even sleep more soundly with a trusted friend by your side. The world literally becomes a safer place with someone you love, and who loves you.

Few things are worse for us emotionally than living with or working with enemies. Too many families conduct themselves as if they were all enemies of each other. Parents, children, siblings, and spouses are then in chronic strife, and families that live this way are so accustomed to it they can't see the problem. Their toxic lifestyle is so familiar it seems normal to them, even if they give insincere lip service to loving one another. Such families are swamped in endless put-downs, challenges to authority and pecking order, betrayals, subterfuge, and passive aggression. Cutting and sarcastic remarks, funny or witty as they may be, can come with the toxic hormones of fight or flight, because the subconscious has no sense of humor. A loving family needs mutual emotional support.

A pattern of family strife, which may have a long history of many generations, needs to be broken and replaced with patterns of trust and support. The stress of chronic fear that comes from living with enemies is profoundly unhealthy and dangerous.

Social connections are necessary for sustainable, fruitful existence. In the next chapter, we discuss in greater detail the general health benefits of love.

Summary of this chapter:

1—There's ample evidence social connections are required for a healthy, happy life. It rates in importance with air, food, and water as a virtual necessity. We seem to know, instinctively, that on a team we are safer and more powerful than alone.

2—When lacking real human connections, we resort to connections with animals, other lonely individuals in cyberspace, or vicarious connections through literature, fantasy, and mass media.

3 —We sometimes pursue negative connections when lacking positive social connections, preferring strife over isolation. But, that has its costs in mental and physical health as well.

4—We don't always know we need to connect with someone when we are alone and starving for such a connection.

5—Past toxic relationships can make us afraid to pursue new relationships, locking us into a cycle of loneliness.

Love and Health

There are many claims about the health benefits of love, affection, and the human and animal touch. Some are exaggerated and wither under harsh skeptical analysis, but strip away the new age and alternative medicine myths, and provable health benefits of loving and being loved remain. It's not so much that love makes you healthy, but rather, love tends to reduce or eliminate the stresses that make you unhealthy.

Stress is unhealthful and will shorten your life, because the stress response that prioritizes fighting immediate threats stops you from healing and maintaining a healthy body. An immediately threatening person needs to be dealt with before longer time scale activities like fighting parasites, healing injuries, or digesting food. People under stress tend develop stomach ulcers because digestive acids linger, and the ulcerating bacteria (*Helicobacter pylori*) aren't fought as hard by the immune system.

Nearly every activity of the body is breaking it down, so it needs to be continuously repaired and built back up. Under stress, the rebuilding and repair functions are put on hold, and under continuous stress, the body will suffer continuous breakdown.

Acute, temporary stress is a natural part of life. Our bodies are tuned to deal effectively with momentary stressors. In fact, we are so well tuned to this that it can actually be healthy to be occasionally stressed. It's why we enjoy roller coaster rides and scary movies. Chronic stress, like enduring a miserable workplace for months or years where your boss threatens to fire you unless you accomplish impossible tasks, can be catastrophic to your health and well-being.

We live in a society of both chronic and acute threats and stress. We can stress for days, weeks, months, or years with little relief, dealing with or worrying about jobs, finances, aggressive family members or neighbors, politics, car troubles—the list is endless. Chronic stress will kill you before your time. It's also been found that stress disrupts the body's normal progression of inflammation, and chronic inflammation can lead to autoimmune diseases like arthritis, brain conditions like dementia, and DNA damage that leads to cancer. Additionally, the body's natural systems that deal with cancer are impaired while you are under social stress. The ways we deal with stress, such as with smoking or drinking, can directly cause yet more health problems. Love, affection, and trust stop the stress cycle by putting us in a situation of perceived safety so our bodies can return to their normal state of healing.

Lacking love, affection, or supportive companionship is something we instinctively know to be itself a threat, and therefore a reason to be stressed. Loneliness often triggers depression, leading to a wide array of self-destructive behaviors. The health threat to individuals, and to society, of loneliness and isolation, is enormous.

We've found a number of ways around the problem of healing while stressed by loneliness. Cuddle therapy services have appeared in recent years where professional cuddlers engage in non-sexual contact for a fee. Therapy dogs have been around for many years, visiting hospital patients, especially children, in social isolation. Even stuffed animals have been used therapeutically in clinical situations.

Then, there's laughter therapy. Journalist Norman Cousins made famous the idea when he claimed watching movie comedies cured him of a crippling illness. What's intriguing about it is that humor can be thought of as a tickling of the mind that repurposes the physiological mechanism of affectionate skin tickling. Being tickled, as long as it's not abusive or unwelcome, is a way to say, "I love you." When our minds are tickled with humor, we respond in a way that's like being tickled physically. It's no wonder, then, that the first thing many women say that they want in a mate is a sense of humor. Laughter therapy has provable health benefits. Cutting or sarcastic humor, interestingly, has the function of social bonding through identifying and agreeing to disparage a common enemy—an unfortunate phenomenon discussed at length in the chapter, "I Love You Because You Hate Who I Hate."

Lack of affection could be the primary cause of addictions (Szalavitz). This includes addictions to substances like heroin or alcohol, taken for some benefit that, once the body adapts, require steadily stronger doses and punishing consequences of withdrawal. It also includes *behavioral* addictions like gambling, sex, junk food, Internet browsing, video games, and shopping. At the hormonal level it turns out substance and behavioral addictions are very much the same in that they both involve the dopamine and endorphins responsible for the misery and compulsion of attempts at withdrawal. While some behavioral addictions are asocial, like slot-machine gambling, they may still get the afflicted out of a lonely house and into a more social setting. The fact that addictions are often linked to social environments hints that loneliness may be their cause.

Important early studies of addiction used solitary rats in cages as test subjects—in "Skinner boxes" where rats could push a lever wired to directly stimulate the pleasure centers of their brains (Olds/Milner 1954). The rats ended up compulsively pushing the button and doing nothing else, quickly killing themselves by forgoing food and drink. What confounded that and similar studies was the researchers disregarded the fact that rats were social animals, and that the rats killing themselves with addictions were alone with nothing else to do. Rats with activities other than directly pleasuring themselves lost interest in the lever and instead behaved normally, enjoying toys, challenges, and companionship. A reasonable conclusion would be that addictions are a result of boredom and loneliness.

People with healthy social lives typically find little interest in addictive activities that others find compelling. Remember also that we can be lonely if we live with or work with or even have sex with people we regard, in our hearts, as enemies (toxic relationships). This is why a person in an emotionally pathological household (socially lonely while not physically alone) can develop most any sort of addiction. There are even cases in recent news of mothers who one could argue are addicted to childbirth and adoption, likely because they live deprived of adequate affection from peers and older children. Couples and families can be physically together but emotionally alone. It's telling that Alcoholics Anonymous's program includes a supportive social collective which restores human connection. Step #8 of their twelve-step program, making amends to those they've harmed, is a gesture one can interpret as turning those they've estranged back into friends and restoring their trust.

A revealing twist of many addictions is that they *enable* social connections, increasing the problem of beating them if they were caused by loneliness to begin with. Addiction to smoking, for example, can put you into a group of people who have nothing in common but meeting at the smoking area same time, same place, and every day. There are social drinkers, gamblers, drug addicts, and sex addicts, who likely began their addictions because of loneliness but, once hooked, associated the addiction even more strongly with the yearning for human connection. Many addictions can be interpreted as failed attempts at alleviating loneliness.

Addictions are overcome not just by avoiding what we are addicted to, but by directly satisfying the hunger that the addiction had likely been replacing—real affection.

Summary of this chapter:

1—Affection and companionship are healthful because they relieve stress, including the stress of loneliness.

2—Under stress, the body's functions of building up after damage or fighting disease are put on hold. The reduction and elimination of stress from being in an affectionate relationship allows these reparative and disease-fighting processes to work at full strength.

3—Humor is healing because it is social play that tickles the brain with the intent to give pleasure, so long as you are not the victim of cutting or sarcastic humor.

4—Social isolation has recently been discovered to be the likely root cause of addictions.

Love Is Indirectly "Selfish," and That's OK

I used to think that a loving relationship was about maxing out my own pleasure. It's not. It's about maxing out your partner's pleasure.

My mother hugged too long, and too hard. She had the mistaken impression that if she showed her affection the way her heart told her to, it would be received as she intended. She was wrong. Without knowing it, she was loving selfishly, because she was not sensitive to how her expressions of love affected those she was loving. Her feelings of affection were deep and sincere, but she thought loving intensely the way she wanted to would be welcomed. It wasn't. She imposed herself on others—not out of passive aggression (hidden anger), but out of misplaced confidence her intent would magically be understood. We are not born with love skills. We often mislearn them and are then deluded into thinking our loving feelings for others will be perceived as intended, and reciprocated.

Everything we do is ultimately selfish, or more precisely, out of self-interest. Even altruism is of self-interest, since we expect our acts of kindness will make us feel good. Altruism is of *indirect* self-interest, and there's nothing wrong with that. It's when we think *only* of ourselves, in how we treat the ones we love, that we make a mess of things. Love is objectionably selfish when it *fails to account for its effects on the person you love.* If you want to be loved in return, your partner must enjoy your acts of love.

We are born prewired at birth to *accept* (receive) love, but must learn by trial and error or teaching how to *give* love. We don't automatically know how to make someone feel good. When someone makes us feel good, we just feel good. That just happens to be the way nature built us. There's little to learn in receiving pleasure. Our world is full of things that make us feel good by virtue of how our DNA has programmed us.

Babies are typically born looking cute and smelling nice. This is how they first make their parents, family, tribe, and strangers feel good. They do not decide to do this. They are programmed to be naturally cute by their DNA, and their family and tribe are similarly programmed to recognize their cuteness. They are born that way, and we are born to appreciate it. They also instinctively desire to suckle, which, not by chance, most mothers also instinctively enjoy, since nipple stimulation results in the production of oxytocin, the love, cuddle, and trust hormone which feels good and helps us to trust whoever or whatever is around us when we feel it. A newborn doesn't really know it's giving pleasure to the mother. It's just hungry, wants hunger pangs relieved, and wants to enjoy the sweet taste of mother's milk. And, mother's milk is supplied instinctively. The baby's first meal is programmed to be a mutual exchange of self-centered pleasure. Mutual trust then comes into play, because the mother's oxytocin assures her this new creature isn't going to eat her, but will instead give her good feelings.

From that comes mutual eye contact and smiling, which helps the baby learn to identify who's making it feel good, as well as the mother. This is the prototype of loving relationships of all types. The message, going both ways, is "we make each other feel good and won't hurt each other."

However, this can go awry. A baby can suckle too strongly and cause pain. A mother can press her baby against her too hard and suffocate it (the buildup of carbon dioxide in the throat is painful). This is where giving love *properly* needs to be learned—when it's not instinctive—and learning is an error-prone, imperfect process confounded by personal delusions and cultural misinformation. For example, babies can be annoying by being demanding, or not developing toilet talents, trying their parents' patience, before they learn good manners. Only maturity from observing their parents' reactions to their behaviors will they begin to understand the importance of not squandering their parents' affections.

It's fine to love selfishly, or rather with self-interest, so long as the self-interest is *indirect*. That is, loving with the expectation to enjoy another person's happiness, and therefore being loved in return. To do this well, we must be aware of how our actions are appreciated. You can inspire someone love you by making them the beneficiary of your friendship, talents, skills, generosity, understanding, and attractiveness.

Summary of this chapter:

1—Loving well is of <u>indirect</u> *self-interest because it's expecting to feel good, yourself, as a result of making your partner feel good.*

2—Loving poorly is <u>directly</u> *selfish. It's placing your own enjoyment of someone ahead of their enjoyment of you. It's to not attend to or care about whether or not your acts of love are enjoyed.*

3—Acting lovingly means loving in ways that make your loved one's enjoyment of your actions your first priority.

4—Build trust by letting those you love know that it's important to you that you make them feel good, and won't make them feel bad.

Learning to Give Love

Angela told me she used to think, while in intimate situations with her ex-boyfriend, "why not just let him keep doing what he thinks feels good to me?" How about, because he won't then ever learn what feels good to you? Or, because his efforts will leave you bored and resentful? Perhaps, because you'll start to think he's an incompetent lover, and lose respect for him? How could he know what feels good to you if you never tell him?

There's a TV commercial about movable car seats showing a mother driving while her kid, in the seat behind her, kicks her seat again and again, repeating, "mom, mom, mom, mom." It's in the commercial because so many parents are familiar with moments like this. The kid obviously wants its mother's love, but is acting in a way that spoils it. This is an example of my argument that we're not born knowing how to love. We tend to act in selfish ways that can squander and damage the love people have for us. We seem to be born rather clueless about this. We have to learn it, and the purpose of this book is to teach us how to love and how to act in ways that create, support, and preserve the love others have for us.

My girlfriend I was deeply in love with, at a beach concert, began to lovingly stroke my knee. She stroked it with love, and I received it lovingly, but she repeated the same stroke on the same spot again and again, until it chafed and hurt. I found myself afraid to ask her to stop, because she was doing it in a loving way and I would have hurt her feelings, so I let her continue. It hurt more and more, and I started to sense resentment rising up inside of me. At an instinctual level, it felt as if she *intended to injure me.* I realized my feelings of affection for her were threatened. Finally, I asked her to stop. If I'd waited for anger to rise up, I could have treated her in a way that seriously threatened our relationship. For the rest of the concert, I felt worried that she was upset, and I didn't know what to do if our nice date had turned sour because of such a seemingly small thing. She'd been giving me love with her warm touch, but unknown to her, I was not receiving it. In other words, what she'd been doing felt bad, not good, and her intent did not override the simple fact that it hurt, and it was she who was hurting me. What I needed to do was stop her, immediately, in a way that didn't hurt *her* feelings. At the time, I was so far from understanding how love worked, it likely played a part in our eventual breakup. She was attempting to give love, but I was not *receiving* it, since my body perceived her actions as inflicting injury. Additionally, my *fear* that she'd be upset when I rejected her affectionate actions could have become another source of discomfort eroding our love. We definitely don't want to be afraid of the person we love. That would amount to a failure of trust.

Love is not enough. Your feeling of love, no matter how strong, has no effect on the world. Only your actions do—love's expression. If your love is not perceived by those you love, it will mean nothing to them and do nothing for them. If you "follow your heart" and approach someone who doesn't trust you, it can be perceived as an attack. Your feelings of love, no matter how strong, won't matter. If someone you love is afraid of you, it will be irrelevant how deeply *you* feel your love. As powerful as those feelings may be to you, by themselves, they have no power in the world unless they are expressed—acted out—in ways that assure the ones you love that you can be trusted.

Love is given through our actions and received through our senses. When one person reaches out to another with the intent to show affection, and the other rejects the gesture, it's a failed attempt to give love. Watch a young toddler try to pet a cat for the first time to see how giving love is not an inborn skill. They often pet the fur the wrong direction, which may feel wonderful to the child but be torture for the cat. An intolerant cat will walk away or possibly attack the clueless child, and in so doing, hopefully begin the child's lessons on how love should and should not be expressed (at least with a cat). Though we are born pre-wired to receive love, much of the time, we need to learn how to *give* love, and *unlearn* habits we may have learned that rub people the wrong way and spoil love.

Our senses pick up what feels good. Our inborn emotional programming interprets another's actions as either beneficial or harmful. We receive love first as infants, from our parents', families', and friends' and neighbors' stroking and soothing touch, voice, and eye contact, and the gifts of milk and food.

Being fed is instinctively interpreted as love. When we are first fed milk as infants, if it comes from our mother, it's received as mother's love. A delicious meal, candy on holidays, going out for ice cream, a birthday or wedding cake, a mixed drink for an attractive stranger at a bar—all are naturally understood as offerings of affection because they engender trust. Candy at Halloween is an implicit message that our neighbors have affection for us and are trustworthy. Candy on Valentine's Day makes the statement, "I feed you especially tasty food."

There are ways in which acts of love can run afoul, however. Love can be received when not given, and can be given but not received, and the reasons include insufficient feedback, projection (thinking someone feels the same as you), and wishful thinking (assuming someone feels good just because you want them to feel good).

We naturally assume what we feel is also felt by who we're with. We have an innate ability to picture another's experience—to feel what others are feeling. A theory from neurology is that we do this in our brains with what are called *mirror neurons*. When we watch someone get hurt, these neurons behave just as if we, ourselves, were being hurt in exactly the same way. When we feel empathetically towards someone, we feel their pain and enjoy their pleasure. It's key to being a loving person, to being good at giving love, to picture your loved one's enjoyment of your actions—to be in their head. This ability, however, is imperfect, and it's the overconfidence we have that love in some way communicates magically that can lead us to not be as good at it as we think we are or want to be. Intentions are not magical. Caressing that's intending to be loving can be received as unpleasant, grating, or painful, regardless of its intent. You might be stroking someone you didn't know had a terrible sunburn under his or her shirt, or a bruise or cut, and an apology may only go so far to remedy the mistake. Our core person, or deep emotional self, may not easily forgive an act that hurts, even with the knowledge that there was no *intent* to hurt.

Summary of this chapter:

1—We are born clueless about how to give love. In fact, we love rather incompetently at first.

2—We may stroke or act affectionately to someone with full intent to please, and fail.

3—Without feedback from those we are trying to please letting us know what's working and what's not, we will never learn to love well.

4—We may assume someone loves us as we love them, just because we want them to. This can be deeply delusional.

5—We need to welcome suggestions from those we love on how to love them better.

The Limits of Honesty

"The one charm of marriage is that it makes a life of deception a necessity."
- Oscar Wilde [6]

Honesty in a relationship is overrated.

Steve had a work assignment that took him away from his girlfriend for several months, during which time they only saw each other on weekends. At the end of the assignment, his girlfriend noticed he was distracted and moody. She insisted he explain what the problem was, with her assurance that she could handle anything. The expectation was that a good relationship would survive any honest revelation. She was mistaken. When Steve told her he'd developed a crush on a woman he'd been working with, she had a terrible panic attack. It was like a stab wound directly to her heart, and they split up shortly thereafter. His honesty about the reason for his moodiness ironically became for her a reason to not trust him, both because his eye had wandered, and because he'd hurt her feelings with the revelation. Holding back the fact of his wandering eye would have left her trust intact. Sharing the fact killed her trust.

I asked a married friend, "suppose you told your wife every morning when you woke up you loved her, and one morning, for whatever reason, you just didn't feel that love? Would you say it anyway?" He admitted he would lie. She'd likely be terrified. The feeling could have come back to him the next morning, but her memory of the morning he didn't say he loved her that caused her fear and pain, may never be forgotten. The morning of the missed "I love you" could have started an erosion of doubt that, over time, could have ended the relationship.

The ideology that one should always be honest in a relationship breaks down when there is a mismatch between honesty of fact and honesty of emotion. Maintaining trust is what's needed to maintain love. It can be a balancing act to reconcile the trust one engenders from being truthful, against being caring and considerate by hiding painful truths that don't really need to be shared. The honesty of the emotional consideration can justifiably trump the honesty of hard facts when the two are in conflict.

We are flawed. A tendency to be attracted to someone other than our mate is natural. Sharing these moments with a loved one, of feeling interested in someone else, is at its heart dishonest because it can function as a threat to a partner who we have no intent to threaten. Honesty of fact can come packaged with a payload, intentional or not, of deceptive emotion. Complete faith in honesty to build trust is misguided.

Honest revelations can also be dishonestly coupled with mismatched emotion as *passive aggression,* where we endeavour to hurt someone in a way that allows us to deny intent to hurt.

We often hear that honesty is a vital part of a successful relationship. Certainly, to find out you've been lied to can erode or quickly destroy trust. However, it's often more important to show honesty of emotion than to state hard facts as if their emotional content was insignificant. The emotional payload of honest but hurtful facts can quickly undermine a trusting relationship.

Is there a more loaded question than, "Do I look fat?" To ask this is to attempt to sabotage a relationship, since any answer can be twisted to appear hurtful. One can even resent being asked such a question, which in itself can be taken as an attack, and therefore, a breach of trust, unless understood as a form of play.

There's a conflict between engendering trust by being honest, and endangering trust by hurting feelings with excessive, careless, or clumsy honesty. You will hear the truth from those who are not afraid to hurt your feelings—but they may not love you at all.

Summary of this chapter:

1—Honesty of emotion often trumps honesty of information.

2—Sharing hurtful truth can be misinterpreted as intent to hurt.

Does Love Die, or Is It Forever?

"Love never dies. It's like a boulder that may be submerged under water. You don't see it, but it's always there."
- Harold "Doc" Humes [7]

Doc Humes gave lots of bad advice, and I disagree with him on this, but there is hidden wisdom in his statement about the permanence of love.

Since love can be defined as the intuitive understanding that someone is good for us, love can die if it's sensed the person we loved will cause us harm. We have in our culture, however, the belief that love is forever.

We all change over time, and if we look closely at events in a fluid relationship we may recognize those that caused the love shared at the beginning to change for one or both partners. Sometimes the change is for the better, or at least harmless, and love lives on. Sometimes, however, divergence can be a tangible threat to the relationship.

Feelings may change even when the people in a relationship don't change. Love is "forever" as long as the memory of someone we once loved lasts. A person you loved that made you feel wonderful in the past, you may think of as a different person now—someone you most certainly do not love in the present. You can forever love the person in your past memories, and not love, even hate, what the person has become.

The promise in the moment of everlasting love is, however, a profound promise of trustworthiness, and there is no intention here to minimize the power of that promise. There are few things more powerfully endearing to *hear* than someone's vow to love you forever, to always be there for you, to always make you feel good, to never make you feel bad, to never cause harm. It's also often called "unconditional" love. The ability to follow through, however, on a promise one's love is "unconditional" is irrelevant.

Failures to meet such a promise are rampant. Failed marriages, relationships, children abandoned for one infraction or another. It's a promise meant to keep yet often broken. It's a promise usually made with perfect sincerity at the time the promise is made, and the chances of succeeding in honoring the promise are beside the point. The intent of the promise is what matters.

Summary of this chapter:

1—There is ample evidence our cultural notion that true love is forever is mere fantasy.

2—What can be considered as the forever part of love is the lasting memory of the loving phase of a relationship's past.

3—The <u>promise</u> *of everlasting, unconditional love, though unrealistic, is a powerful foundation for deep affection.*

Creating New Love

In some versions of *Aladdin and the Magic Lamp* the Genie has a rule that he can't make someone fall in love. That's a storytelling device setting up Aladdin to earn the Princess's love legitimately. It also exploits the belief many have that there is an existing soulmate we just have to somehow find. Many assume true love can't be engineered, but it can, indeed, be earned.

Can you "make" someone love you? That's a very strong word, since it sounds like you'd be forcing someone to feel or do something against their will. Let's soften it to this: How would you inspire someone to love you who presently didn't—to give it your best shot? Assure them, without being too obvious about it, that they can trust you will always make them feel good and never make them feel bad, that you are always on their side and you will never betray them, that you will never hurt them, you will be there for them, you are honest, and that being with you is safe—safe from strife, from pain, from conflict, and that you can be relied upon. That applies to common love like friendship, affection, and companionship, but what about romantic love?

Aside from sexual attraction, which is covered in the next chapter: "Affectionate Sex, Hateful Sex," the deep and lasting love one creates with a romantic partner comes from a blend of opposites: similarity and difference. We are comfortable around people who are like ourselves, but we also want to be around people different in ways that we admire and are therefore interesting rather than just comfortable. Too similar is dull. Too different is frightening. The blend has to be just right.

Now, we often hear that "opposites attract" as if personal attraction followed the same laws of physics as electricity and magnetism. It's sometimes used to explain couplings of a blonde with a brunette, an athlete with a scholar, a rich person and a poor person, tall with short, slim with full-figured, and so on. These are not really *opposites*. They are *differences*. A blonde is not the opposite of a brunette. Instead, we are attracted to aspects of mates which we admire and *don't have in ourselves*, so it's not typical, for instance, for a natural blonde to be attracted to blondes. It's even applicable to sexual attraction. Heterosexual men are attracted to female physiques and personalities because they are different from their own, *and* are considered admirable, and likewise for what women find attractive in men. Even in homosexual relationships, it's differences that attract. This principle works at nearly every level of mating, from the fundamental molecular level, to the anatomical, intellectual, and cultural levels. We are instinctively sexually attracted to people who have genes different from ours in the hopes that they will be added to our own genes, endowing our offspring with an advantage. Too little or too much genetic difference between fertile partners can lead to congenital problems in offspring. Great cultural and ideological differences can lead to conflicts and inconsistencies in parenting, and in other ways destabilize a happy, passionate relationship.

So, to generate and maintain romantic affection, one would appreciate the similarities in one's partner, as well as the differences. It's as if to say, "we work together for a common goal, and I can help us in this way you can't, and you can help us in this other way I can't."

Finally, here's a followup to the discussion in the previous chapter about everlasting love. We should promise, when the time is right, to unconditionally and forever love the one we'd like to love us. That feeling and belief are real, *wonderfully real*, but it's a promise that is in practice delusional and unfulfillable, as the many breakups and betrayals attest. What matters is *believing* it. Unconditional, everlasting love is the heart's smoke and mirrors magic trick. It's the basis of the human bond, because it's about expecting safety in a relationship, or, expecting that we can trust that the one we love will not leave us or turn against us.

And also, it's terribly important when establishing trust to avoid triggering fear in the person you wish will love you—a principle that applies to all types of newly-minted loving and affectionate relationships.

Summary of this chapter:

1—You'll be loved by people who feel safe with you and are sure you are good for them.

2—Romantic love involves a blend of similarities and differences, since we like to be with someone who is like ourselves, but also like to be with someone who has attributes we admire that we do <u>not</u> have in ourselves. Too similar is dull, but too different is threatening.

3—A promise of everlasting, unconditional love is a powerful generator of deep affection—unrealistic, but it's the thought that counts.

Affectionate Sex, Hateful Sex

There really does seem to be two categories of sex: love-sex and hate-sex.

Love-sex finds pleasure in giving pleasure—in enjoying vicariously the pleasure your partner receives from you. Hate-sex takes pleasure without regard for the experience of your partner, or worse, taking pleasure from your partner's displeasure. Why these both exist is likely connected with the essential duality of interpersonal relations—seeing individuals as friend or foe.

Hate-sex tends to focus on the erogenous zones, love-sex on the whole partner. Hate-sex objectifies and seeks to *take* pleasure from the other. Love-sex seeks to *give* pleasure and celebrates the partner's whole person. Hate-sex doesn't care about the partner's pleasure. Love-sex takes pleasure in the partner's pleasure.

The phenomenon is observable in nature in a way that parallels, and manifests, the same pattern

101

in human relationships. Without all the human complications, we can more easily, in animals, see the meaning and purpose of natural behaviors and tendencies.

Sex between non-social animals is very much like the hate-sex we're discussing. Normally they avoid each other and fight for territory and threaten to maim or kill each other unless the compulsion to exchange DNA during the mating season brings about a kind of truce just for the sex act. The male only wants to take pleasure from the female, and short of outright rape, will try to impress the female into compliance with a show of one kind of strength or another. The female will *want* to be impregnated by a male of strength because of the chance that genes responsible for his strength will be inherited by her offspring. There are many ways males show strength, from demonstrations of talents to the strength to overcome female resistance. A male strong enough to overcome an unwilling female's resistance may very well result in offspring with the same strength, somewhat depressingly rendering that advantage to the offspring. His overwhelming dominance, paradoxically, can be an experience of ecstatic enjoyment for his unwilling victim. Nature is not politically correct.

Social animals like ourselves, on the other hand, can have sex with lasting love and affection. Love-sex, unlike hate-sex, is about giving, not taking. It plays a part in pair bonding, which is immensely valuable to mating individuals, and therefore, to the offspring resulting from the act.

The function of hate-sex is to couple momentarily for the sole purpose of getting off, and afterwards, to revert to disinterested antagonism. Barren estrangement often follows the ecstasy of the hate-sex act. The sequence of feelings follows instinctive programming that gives little to no clue for the participants as to the reason those feelings are there. Ecstasy is followed by revulsion. Delicious, sometimes to the point of addiction while one's doing it, then toxic in its aftermath. Even though the capacity for hate-sex is innate, it's better to avoid it because the toxicity that follows the act, the bitter loneliness and failed fulfillment, too often outweighs and outlasts its brief bliss.

Love-sex, on the other hand, is not followed by a toxic aftermath. The pleasure can last because it's about making a lasting bond that keeps you in cooperative pairs to help each later in the parenting cycle. Oxytocin flow is prolonged by the cuddling during afterglow. It's good for you in the long term. It's why people in lasting marriages live longer, at least marriages that are affectionate and supportive, and not adversarial.

Summary of this chapter:

1—Hate-sex, angry, or uncaring sex, seeks to <u>take</u> *pleasure from your partner.*

2—Love-sex endeavors to <u>give</u> *pleasure to your partner.*

3—Hate-sex is likely an instinctive reproductive strategy that, as a side effect, contributes to making the world less loving than it could be.

4—To avoid the toxic aftermath of hate-sex, we can choose love-sex, keeping hate-sex in the realm of occasional play-acting if not avoiding it altogether.

What Threatens Love

Studies show you are 40% more likely to have your marriage end in divorce if your parents were divorced. I grew up in a family in which we didn't care if we hurt each other's feelings.

Consider this parable of nature:

A mother bird builds a nest pretty much like the nest her mother built: In a similar tree, surrounded by similar smells, sounds, and sights, using her memories from her own infancy as a guide. The nest she grew up in was good enough, since, there she is, becoming a mother herself. As she builds her nest, however, she by chance doesn't notice a twig she added that had particularly sharp thorns. When her eggs hatched, some of her chicks were badly cut by the thorns. Most died, but a single chick managed to make it to adulthood in spite of her injuries. When that chick grew up and became fertile and started to make her own nest, she recalled the thorny twig in the nest she was raised in, and being too young at the time to recall how it injured her and her siblings, just didn't think her new nest looked right unless a similarly thorny twig was included in the one she was building. She instinctively duplicated a feature from her infancy that was harmful to her, and would be harmful to *her* chicks, merely because it was *familiar*. In a kind of misguided nostalgia, she took it on faith that what she grew up with was good. She laid her eggs, and they hatched, but her chicks were then harmed by the thorns. Some died, and the ones that survived, if any, grew up to again feel certain that a thorny twig was a requirement of a proper nest. Family pathologies are passed down from generation to generation. They are persistent and even fiercely defended because they are familiar and just *feel* right.

So, if you're wondering why you are having the same problems in your relationships that your parents had which led to their unhappiness or divorce, the answer is, you are likely unknowingly duplicating the thorns from your parent's nest in the nest you are building—familiar thorns you mistakenly thought were harmless and normal, or maybe even thought were beneficial, that you fiercely defended.

Paula's family group, which consisted of a father, son, grandmother, mother, and daughter, had a habit of subjecting its male members to frequent ridicule. It was their family culture. Every meal had to include a reminder of the father's or son's stupidity or incompetence. This was thought of as innocent family fun, though it in fact eroded the happiness of the men and boys. It inevitably also bounced back to degrade the emotional quality of life for the women as well. The younger boy had to learn to get used to this. At his youngest, when he first realized he was being ridiculed, he cried, fought back, and made scenes, all of which were seen as confirmation, for the mother and girls, of how foolish he was. In time, he learned to accept it, partly by observing how his father also accepted being ridiculed, and ultimately assumed it was a normal aspect of family life. In spite of the boy's acclimation to being a daily target of ridicule, it created stress and squandered family love, support, and unity all the way up to maturity and emancipation. Some boys suffering through this would fall off an emotional cliff and never recover normal self-esteem. The ones that did grow up to start families of their own would pick a mate who had a similar style of ridiculing males. All he'd have to do is make some strategic mistake on the first date, she'd pounce and ridicule, and he'd get that familiar feeling of "I know this—it feels like family," and the thorns that took down his siblings and nearly took him down, he would begin to build into his own nest.

The genders in the above story can be flipped and the point we are making here would be the same. A family in which men constantly demeaned women will result in men who feel they are entitled to it, and women who accept it as normal family culture to be passed down to the next generation. Again, the same result follows: erosion of family affection and cohesion. Additionally, it generates the toxic stress at critical points in childhood development from living with someone who, at a deep and real emotional level, is an enemy.

The ways we love poorly are infinite, but they all follow the same theme—to make the person you love feel bad, physically or emotionally. It's to put them on the wrong side of the friend or foe duality via a toxic power struggle.

We need our parents, children, siblings, mates, co-workers, customers, and vendors to see us as friend and not foe. It's hard to change what we've learned from childhood and taken for granted. If we want to love well, and enjoy the health and well-being of loving relationships with friends and family, we need to invest in the effort to see the unhealthy habits we've learned from our youth for what they are, to stop defending them, and to live our lives in different and better ways.

If you've grown up in a family that didn't love well, you need to stop saying "I turned out fine" to justify continuing toxic traditions, and embrace a new way of treating others and interpreting how others treat you.

Being born into a family that is emotionally or physically abusive is quite literally being taken hostage. We depend on our abusers for food and shelter, are afraid of their bullying, and may end up defending the abuse and becoming abusers ourselves.

It's been said that contempt is the number one predictor of a marriage's failure (relationship expert Dr. John Gottman). While contempt for one's spouse has a long history in American and some other cultures, the explosive popularity of television in the 1950s powerfully influenced the attitudes of millions. A case in point is a hugely successful sitcom which ran from 1951 to 1957 and was watched by fifty million people, about one third of America.

The running joke of the popular and award-winning *I Love Lucy* television show was how contemptuously Lucy and Desi treated each other, the implication being that their love was so strong, it survived their hateful, conniving, dishonest conduct and eye-rolling mutual disgust. Television is replete with all manner of appealing but unrealistic fantasies. Audiences like the idea that one can treat one's spouse horribly, and true love will still win in the end, but it's a huge lie too much of America bought into. Divorce rates soared, and copycat sitcoms, portraying unrelenting contempt between husband and wife, were epidemic and remain so to this day. The Lucy show was not unique, and contempt in domestic relationships in the popular arts, traceable to ancient Greece, became ever-present for baby boomers in shows like *The Honeymooners, Home Improvement,* and *Roseanne.* The acceptance in our culture of the poison of spousal contempt, and the belief that it's not harmful to relationships, is appalling.

Consciously we know these shows are fiction, but a constant barrage of this type of fiction can result in subconscious or semiconscious acceptance and approval of verbal cruelty. It's doubtless that many people, especially younger people, imprint on stereotypes of toxic relationships they see in fiction and start to think it's acceptable, normal, or even "cool" to verbally abuse one's partner.

We have to stop and say, "no, this is not a good model for a relationship, and I will not engage in contempt for my husband, wife, children, or parents." Relationships erode, not survive, in an atmosphere of mutual contempt. Making it comical hardly mitigates this, because the subconscious has no sense of humor. The real-world marriage between Lucy and Desi Arnez ended catastrophically in physical abuse and infidelity which very likely echoed what was portrayed so humorously and seemingly harmlessly on their program.

Conflict between lovers or between parents is not the only process in which toxic feuding can sabotage love for subsequent generations. When resources are limited, siblings can turn against each other, and, of course, a stronger sibling has a greater chance of survival if it eliminates a weaker sibling. Families can fall into cruel pecking orders, often determined by birth order, that are not only quite toxic to the youngest in the family, but by transference will be echoed in the children's later adult relationships. That is, an older, bullying child can grow up to be a bullying lover, mother, or father, transferring the feelings and behavior they practiced towards their younger siblings to their adult partners. That way, it can subsequently become like the thorn in the nest they grew up in, which they will build in their own future nest. When parents adopt a hands-off policy to hateful conflicts between their children, it's likely to not just erode the affection needed in the family, but to again become a habit passed down to subsequent generations. Parents who witness the emergence of toxic conflict between their children need to assertively act to persuade them that their lives will be better today, tomorrow, and for the rest of their lives if they learn to love their siblings and not get locked into hate. They need to be encouraged to see each other as friends to cooperate with, not enemies to conquer. Backing off and letting them "work it out for themselves" can allow it to escalate into real and permanent physical and emotional damage.

The threats jealousy and rivalry pose to family serenity are the subject of the next chapter.

Summary of this chapter:

1—We instinctively build a nest for our family like the one we grew up in, duplicating its good and bad features.

2—A thorn in the nest we were brought up in could be a family habit of disparaging one another, cruelly and inconsiderately, in a toxic and unloving environment we duplicate, possibly even magnify, in the family we later raise our own children.

3—For love and affection to thrive, we need to treat the ones we care about as friend and not foe—to make them feel good and not feel bad. If we were raised in a family that failed at this, toxic interactions feel "right" to us, and we repeat the mistakes.

4—The portrayal of contemptuous relationships in mass media, especially television shows like I Love Lucy *and* The Honeymooners, *may have raised a generation that considered family contempt to be harmless fun, when research has shown it's a reliable predictor of divorce.*

5—We can also transfer a toxic, bullying childhood relationship with a sibling to a similarly toxic, bullying adult relationship with a spouse.

6—Toxic family relationships need to be confronted and unlearned to prevent such habits from being passed on to the next generation.

Jealousy, Rivalry, and Living With the Enemy

"The jealous are troublesome to others, but a torment to themselves."
-William Penn [8]

A water ride at a local amusement park made riders so wet they could have jumped over their heads in a swimming pool with their clothes on and ended up just as soaked. A college-age couple on a double date at the ride's exit was very happy until the man looked at his date and saw her T-shirt had become transparent enough to easily see her breasts and nipples. He flew into an inconsolable rage, cursing her and calling her a whore and many more unrepeatable names, surrounded by horrified families trying to shield their youngest from his cruel, blood-curdling rant. "Everyone can see you, you whore!" he screamed again and again. She was, of course, mortified. Innocent of any improper behavior, it's impossible to imagine their relationship surviving the incident. His extreme rage came from an instinctive, unthinking, irrational fear that he would lose her to another man. Ironically, acting out his jealousy that way likely led to her leaving him out of fear his behavior would be triggered repeatedly in their future, and possibly violently. This was not the happy ending to what they'd hoped had been a fun date, but the upside was she got an early warning of what could turn out much worse for her later in the relationship. Was her date triggered to a panic because he'd lost someone he loved in the past who'd flirted with another man? Possibly, but jealousy is deep in our nature. It triggers rage. The reason is that close companionship is so valuable that the panic from the fear of loss is strong enough result in self-defeating aggression and suffocating possessiveness. From our unthinking, instinctive understanding of the tremendous value of a deep connection with a loved one comes the terrifying possibility of its loss.

We naturally want to take it out on our significant other who shows interest in someone outside the relationship because it's potential betrayal.

Jealousy can be in play in almost any kind of relationship, because we're instinctively programmed to feel a trusting relationship is too valuable to risk losing without a fight. The fear of the loss of a trusted friend can be intense. A wife can be jealous of her husband's friendship with his mother. Siblings can be jealous of each other's closeness to a parent. A father can be jealous of his wife's closeness to his son. There is no end to the possible combinations of jealousy in relationship triangles, and when it results in destructive anger, it can add a thorn to the family nest handed down to uncountable future generations (discussed in the previous chapter "What Threatens Love"). Jealousy is understandable, but often irrational and self-defeating.

Sibling rivalry is a special case of jealousy. In competing for a parent's affection, a household that should be a safe haven of tranquility and support can become an emotionally toxic and even physically dangerous war zone. Allowing fighting siblings to "work it out for themselves" makes a family like a pit fight. There are few things worse than being trapped with an arch enemy, and it's tragic how many families permit their kids' home lives to be relentless battle zones. It normalizes conflict and stress in a way that can sabotage hopes for healthy family life for many generations to come.

There's a huge cost in the stress of living with an enemy. If you're used to living that way, you need to awaken to the fact of its toxicity, then resolve to refuse letting it continue. The people close to us—parents, children, siblings, coworkers, and neighbors, need to be cultivated as friends, not enemies. The benefits of a family of peace and love are too great to neglect or dismiss. It's a discipline to go against what we're used to from past family experiences, and against the self-destructive parts of our nature, but it's worth the effort. A family that raises successful, happy and healthy kids is one of love, support, growth, and health, not of distrust, conflict, and toxic stress. Kids need to understand that their siblings' mutual affection, support, and trust is too valuable to waste on petty conflicts. The cycle of the acceptance of living with the enemy must be stopped, because if it continues, it infects and degrades every aspect of our lives.

Don't accept situations of living with an enemy. The chronic stress will kill you.

The last chapters discussed some of the ways love can be lost. The next chapter suggests some ways love can be regained.

Summary of this chapter:

1—An intimate relationship is so valuable that the fear of losing it can result in self-defeating jealous rage and possessiveness.

2—We lash out at our partner in situations of infidelity because the partner is the individual who betrays us.

3—Cruel jealousy within families can turn what should be a safe, loving environment into a toxic war zone.

4—Stopping the cycle of jealous family discord is a discipline well worth the effort for the benefit of future generations.

Restoring Lost Love

Reassure the partner you are afraid you'd lost that you are friend, not enemy, and are trustworthy.

Betty was furious John had flirted with a very pretty girl at the club. They'd been dating for months and had been very affectionate, but now Betty wouldn't let John touch her—pushing his hands away when he reached out to her. John looked at the floor and told her, in a cold, insincere tone, that he was sorry. "No, you're not," she responded. John panicked and said, tearfully, how much he loved her and how sorry he was, then burst into sobbing. She reached out to hold him, and they held each other. He repeated how sorry he was, heaving and shuddering. She felt wet tears on her cheek, took in their distinct scent, tasted them when she kissed his cheek, and she also started to cry. "I'm so sorry I hurt you," he sobbed. "I won't do it again," and she answered that it was OK. They kissed and made love.

One of the best ways to restore someone's love is to cry in front of them. Crying is misunderstood in our culture. Do we cry when we're sad? Then, what's up with so-called tears of joy? Seemingly contradictory types of events can make us cry. Our culture just doesn't get it, but there are clues. The answer is revealed by what hormones are doing when we are in tears.

My first clue about this was when I burst into tears at the end of the Gulf War of 1990-91. This was a terrifying time, with night-vision bombings of Baghdad carried on television every day. On the first day of the fighting, there was a power outage at my workplace, and I thought we'd been thrust into global war. While the battle of Baghdad was raging, I'd hardened my heart against the fear of domestic terror. When the fighting ended, my body no longer needed the fear hormones, so it flushed them from my bloodstream through the tear ducts. I didn't cry when the war began or when the tragedies were reported, but I did cry when it was announced over. Why?

What's fascinating about crying is it does more than help switch off the stressful state of fight or flight. It communicates to those around us that we are making that switch. It tells whoever's there that we no longer want to fight—that we want to make up. If we are crying because of what has been happening in our relationship, it's to show our partner we are switching from foe to friend, or, from fear to trust, or from fear of loss to acceptance of loss. We cry when our bodies want to quickly dump stress hormones (Sapolsky), and show this to others.

Love is usually lost when trust is lost. Biologically, that means someone we thought to be a friend became a non-friend or enemy. We typically say our heart has been broken if we are betrayed by someone we love. Trust can, hopefully, be restored, but there's no guarantee. Zeroing in on how the biology of love and trust works can reveal strategies for winning back love that's been lost—strategies to mend a broken heart.

Love will be lost if the one who had loved you stops trusting you to make them feel good, but instead fears you will hurt them or make them feel bad. If you know what the problem is you can try to manage it. For example, if you learn that hygiene issues have made you unattractive, you can improve your hygiene habits and be open, honest, and reassuring to your loved one that you're dealing with the issue and can be trusted to turn over a new leaf. This can't guarantee recovery of trust, especially if you've reneged in the past, but it gives you your best chance.

Reassurance you've become newly trustworthy is the template for how to plan practically any attempt to restore lost love.

Let's suppose your partner doesn't trust your driving and is afraid of being maimed or killed in an accident. Fear, our most powerful emotion, is profoundly unpleasant. If you truly love your partner, you won't want to be the cause of their fear. If your partner is afraid of your driving, then at a deep level in your partner's heart you are seen as enemy, not friend. Study safe driving, apologize, and assure them you'll drive safely from now on. Seal the deal with a hug and some honest tears and an apology, and don't screw it up by returning to your old, dangerous ways. Your relationship is more valuable than your ego.

Each situation works pretty much the same way. Someone who loves you expects you to make them feel good. Now you are making them feel bad. They've pulled away from you. To bring them back, find out what made them feel bad and reassure them you'll change.

Another method for restoring lost love is with the "different person" template. Someone who loved you, but no longer does, has likely not lost the *memory* of when they loved you. To them, the person they presently don't love is not the same person they loved in the past. Using that model, you can endeavor to return to being the person they previously loved, and stop being the person that squandered their love. An example of this would be if you suddenly started drinking heavily in a relationship that had been successful for some time while you were dry. Drunkenness sometimes changes one's personality so profoundly that, in your partner's eyes, you became a different person from the person you were before you started your drinking habit. By stopping the excessive drinking, you can go back to being the person your partner once loved.

The "different person" model is powerful because distrust is likely permanently associated with a specific person. The memory of betrayal has tremendous persistence because it is of vital importance for us to protect ourselves from repeated betrayal. If you can persuade the one you want to love you again that you are no longer the person who betrayed them, you stand a chance of reviving their love. Oh, and while you are persuading them you are a different person, hold them and let the tears flow. Since crying is one way we rid ourselves of stress hormones, it's good for you and good for the people you cry with, because it tells them you are softening your heart and no longer want to fight or fear.

Summary of this chapter:

1—Crying signals, especially to the ones you want to forgive you, that you do not see them as enemy any longer. It's a way the body breaks down stress hormones, which are then literally secreted in your tears, signalling to those around you that you don't want to fight and that you've softened your heart. It communicates that, for you, the struggle is over.

2—To restore lost love, find out what bothered the person you want to love you again, stop doing that, and assure them that they can trust you to not revert to your old ways. This is often not easy. Each instance depends on what you've done to damage the affection, how you've done it, and how forgiving and motivated your loved one is, but it gives you your best chance.

3—Love is restored by ridding yourself and your partner of the "fight-or-flight" stress hormones, then re-triggering the love hormones with affectionate touch, hugs, and reassurance.

Animal Love

Merlyn taught life-lessons to the child Arthur by turning him into various animals in T. H. White's *The Once and Future King*. We can learn much from watching animals and imagining their perspectives on life and love.

Picture a frozen night in an ice-age cave—a human family huddled around a fire. A wolf pup, abandoned by its pack because of a shortage of food, cautiously approaches the mouth of the cave, attracted by the warmth, the soothing voices of the family's conversations, and the smell of cooking meat. The pup sees the group and is reminded of the pack it misses. Once eye contact is made, it poses in the cutest way it can as if begging to be adopted. The family, overwhelmed by its cuteness, allows it to come near and cuddle. The pup is offered a scrap of food and the deal is sealed—a food offering being a signal of trust as surely as if it had come from the pup's own mother. Oxytocin surges in everyone. The collaboration between the furless and the furry is born.

It turned out to be a good deal for both species. The wolves in human groups were fed and protected, and in exchange, they loved and defended their cave hosts and collaborated in hunting. A tribe that didn't have a wolf's support was no match for one that did, and the wild wolves without human direction faced their own struggles.

Female wolves in heat that lived with cave people at first wandered out to be impregnated by wild wolves—seduced by each other's scents—to return home and spawn pups. The pups that grew to adulthood and benefitted their tribes were allowed to breed with other domesticated wolves. Those that didn't help their tribe were banished or killed. Over many generations, the selectively bred wolves became more and more useful—a process that continues today not just with wolves, but with all domesticated animals.

The relationship proved so beneficial to wolves for so long that there are now an estimated half a billion of them descended from the first few that befriended humans, while those that didn't—the wild wolves—perennially face extinction. Of course, we call our wolf companions dogs, and we've bred them to be useful to us just as we've selectively bred cows and goats and chickens and bananas to our liking. Dogs protect us, hunt for us, love us—and we love them.

This story of wolves and cave people is a simplification, and imagines details unfortunately lost in time. We can't be sure of the specifics, but something very much like what's described here must have happened.

The story of cats is different. It's likely the first cats that moved in with us were exploiting the rat infestations after we started farming and storing grain, about 10,000 years ago in the Near East. We love their soft fur, and a cat's powerful response to petting is an echo of their mother's licking from their kitten stage.

Emotionally, humans are quite a lot like most other mammals, so we can have tremendous affinity for them—especially the social ones—as they can for us. The parts of the human brain involved in emotions, like love, are variations on common animal themes. Horses, dogs, mice, rabbits, and cows share with us the same spectrum of deep feelings and hormones of trust, affection, love, and fear. Once an animal is convinced we are not their predator, prey, or competitor, but a source of food-sharing and affection, the animal can be domesticated. What they then feel for us is real love.

We come into the world needing, indeed demanding, affection. The urge babies feel to cuddle is tremendous, because it's essential for their survival to make alliances with parents, siblings, and tribe-mates. They do it by seeking the pleasure of family and tribal connections.

Our inborn potential to bond with animals is proven by the attraction children have for stuffed animals. Psychologist Harry Harlow, in his classic experiments, showed that infant rhesus monkeys preferred to cuddle with inert puppet mothers covered with soft cloth instead of metal wire ones that gave them milk. When hungry, they visited the metal mother only to feed, then returned to the soft cloth doll. Nearly all mammals need, and intensely enjoy, cuddling with someone or something they trust and expect will make them feel good. It's a myth that animals are in friendships with us only for food.

We can't ultimately know what animals feel, but because of all the biological mechanisms of love we share with them, there's good reason to assume that animal feelings of love are much like our own. Some animals may even feel love *more deeply* than we do. Cats and dogs certainly feel love intensely.

There's huge variety in the animal kingdom. Some mammals are nonsocial hermits when not mating or raising their young, but wolf pack cohesion is manifested in individual dogs as love. While dogs see themselves as members of their human owners' packs, domesticated cats are instead kept in their kitten state for their entire lives and interact with us as if we were their parents. It's not just chance that the two most popular domesticated animals, cats and dogs, are skilled, heartless predators. Extra intensity of the oxytocin effect is needed in predators to suppress their killer instincts for social cooperation, so they likely feel love especially deeply toward their parents, offspring, packmates, peers, and, if successfully domesticated, their human owners.

In the next chapter we discuss how affection for our coworkers, bosses, and subordinates is important to a well-functioning workplace—a setting which echoes the lifestyle and social functions of primitive cave tribes and wolf packs.

Summary of this chapter:

1—The social/emotional biology of animals is similar to ours and serves the same functions, so they likely feel love much as we do.

2—Animal love illustrates the essential principles of human love, because animals' emotional lives are not confounded by the complications of human affairs and cultures.

3—Affection between different animal species is common, because their love biologies are similar, and the loving relationships between us and our household pets demonstrates this.

4—Since love, via its hormone oxytocin, suppresses the predatory killer instinct, the intensity of love that cats and dogs feel for us, and for each other, is likely greater than that of non-predatory pets, like rabbits and hamsters.

I Love My Team Members

Phil Jackson, the legendary basketball coach, said in his book *Eleven Rings* that the most essential ingredient for a team to win an NBA championship was love.

At every job I've had at a large corporation, it was vitally important to me and everyone I worked with to agree on who was a good guy, who was a bad guy, and what clique to align with. Joining a cool, competent clique was a critical mission. Once aligned, I participated in the support of other members of my clique and was encouraged to disparage, shun, and sabotage others. Enjoying the favor of the in-crowd was so valuable that one couldn't risk breaking ranks and not participating in the coordinated subterfuge against rivals. New hires were subtly vetted, romanced if they were deemed cool or skillful, or shunned if they were not. At one firm, every morning about 10:00 AM, we went to our floor's coffee urn where we would freely discuss the intrigue of the day—unless someone from an enemy clique would come by. Then, we were circumspect in stiff politeness. Our managers would ignore it if one group was undermining another group's project, which seemed to have only one explanation: it's how they got to their positions and continued to advance, all the way up the ladder to the top. Because everyone was accustomed to it, few saw how destructive it was to the company's success. They saw it as an admirable sign of a group's determination to win.

It was also an unstable environment where people jumped ship from losing teams, turned against one another, pretended to be on the side of their team while plotting to join a rival team, mutiny, or otherwise betray their team to get ahead.

The culture of intracompany negative competition can't possibly benefit the firm. A few companies have even make cutthroat competition between divisions official policy—with catastrophic results (Kimes).

Returning to Phil Jackson's strategy of using love to build winning teams—you have to love a team member to want to throw them the ball to let *them* make the shot and get the point. Why? Because we're human, not mechanical, and helping our team members, especially in the heat of a game, requires motivation from our deeper, more spontaneous emotional core—not from "thinking" or strategizing. The emotions of quick-acting gameplay need to be aligned with the team's goals. The emotion needed for team cooperation is *love* because it's seeing someone on your team as a cooperator, not a competitor. You trust your teammate to catch your pass and make the shot.

They trust you will pass it to them if that's better for your team than trying to make the shot yourself when you're not well-positioned. A team in which there's no love between players is a team with impaired cooperation, and a team without intuitive teamwork will lose more games than it should.

Lack of cooperation, negative competition, and downright sabotage are endemic to many workplaces, and are not unknown in team sports. Leaders need to detect and eliminate this source of dysfunction, but may not if undermining others was the way they achieved their leadership positions. They are like people who grew up in toxic families and then, as parents themselves, don't condemn it because they see the syndrome's familiarity but not its dysfunction. It's a big step from assuming familiar toxic ways of sports or business teams are normal—to recognizing their harm, but a step a successful company or sports team must take.

Summary of this chapter:

1—Picking friends and enemies at the workplace is a prevalent aspect of unofficial corporate culture, but works against smooth team functioning, so is counterproductive to a company's success.

2—A toxic workplace needs to be recognized by workers and managers at all levels, and must be discouraged by helping everyone on a team, and throughout the company, to see each other as friend and not foe, and to reject clique culture and intra-company hostile competition.

I Love My Dentist

Dr. Payne was the first dentist I was taken to as a child. I'm not kidding. That was his actual name. It was normal then to drill without administering an anesthetic, so it was also normal to hate your dentist. Dr. Payne didn't seem to care that he hurt us.

In my teen years, we moved to another town and switched to a dentist who cared deeply about not hurting his patients. He used masterful techniques to numb us. He even knew how to painlessly inject the painkiller—a typically excruciating moment. He asked us to assure him we were not suffering, and expertly sensed when we were in pain so he could adjust his treatment. We loved him because we could tell he cared about not hurting us.

The intimacy of being worked on so closely, as if being groomed, was not compromised by any neglect for our comfort. We also trusted that our dentist did exactly what was necessary for the

133

quality care of our teeth. This resulted in little doses of oxytocin from the intimate contact that would make it natural for us to say, "I love my dentist."

The dentist experience fits neatly into the thesis of this book. You'll love who you expect to make you feel good rather than bad. My dentist always left us with the message that if we experienced any pain from our teeth, we were to come in and he would take care of it. While there, we knew the agenda was to make us as comfortable as possible and for the visit to be pain-free. Accidental pain or discomfort was understood to be unintentional, as long as it was rare, so it didn't damage the relationship.

The advantage for the *practitioner* of this style of dentistry is great because patients will likely return for repeat business, be less prone to cancel, and maybe even accept higher prices. A caring dentist will be in the "expensive, but worth it" class.

The principle of healing without pain, especially with an affectionate human touch, is applicable to all of the healing arts.

Summary of this chapter:

1—One's relationship with one's dentist has an intimacy that can succeed or fail depending on whether or not one is confident the practitioner will relieve rather than inflict pain.

2—Painless dentistry can be interpreted instinctively as a type of grooming that may result in patients experiencing hormones of affection.

3—A dentists who in their practice makes his or her patients experience hormones of affection is more likely to have a successful practice than one who doesn't, all else being equal.

4—The principle of how painless dentistry can trigger the release of hormones of affection can apply to any healing art involving close physical contact.

Our Loneliness Epidemic

Why are we so damned lonely?

Living alone is at an all-time high. We interact on computer, pad, and phone screens, chatting and blogging and skyping and catfishing, reaching out for the affection we are so hungry for, but futility, because computer social networks lack the physical touch we need to complete the true human connection, and the result is all manner of addictions and obsessions.

Artificial online companionship has a number of pitfalls. One is the risk of idealization of characteristics of online companions not experienced in the medium. For example, if we only text with someone, we can imagine them to be terrific in any other way we need them to be outside the tiny text window. If we only talk with someone by phone we don't see, feel, or smell them. If we see only a head shot, we don't know their body, and so on, and so forth. We imagine what we don't see is what we want to see, and can fall victim to our own wish-fulfilling idealizations.

Then, there's the supernormal stimulus of fictional characters and situations. We watch socially slick people in movies and television shows, or ultra-attractive models in print, commercials, or romantic/erotic videos. We may listen to syrupy, sentimental love songs. All this *desensitizes* us against what's realistic. If we're saturated with unattainable ideals, then the attainable will likely disappoint. It feeds but fails to satisfy our essential hunger for full interaction with real people. Overindulgence in fantasy can lead us to conclude that it's better to be with partly or wholly imaginary friends or lovers than to be with real ones who disappoint us by comparison.

Of course, being alone may be better for us than being with someone who's bad for us. When we spend time with toxic family, friends, or lovers, we get few of the benefits of affection.

The next chapter explores how our need to get along with each other is essential to life itself.

Summary of this chapter:

1—In many societies, loneliness is a spreading epidemic.

2—We seek, futilely, to satisfy our hunger for affection when we seek it online or in other media.

3—Too many of us settle for toxic relationships that are even worse for us than being alone.

Life's Circle of Love

We are born to love because we are social animals. Our first mission in life is to establish trusting, intimate relationships with others.

First with our mothers, then our parents, then our family and its animal companions, our mates in reproduction, and finally, as parents ourselves with our own children and hopefully with their children as grandparents. It's all done via the simple formula of making the ones you love trust that you will make them feel good and not make them feel bad. The most important piece of our natural love machinery is the love/trust hormone, which switches off our fear of one another and switches on our trust. This chapter follows what makes this hormone flow, and what its effects are on body and mind in the span of a generation.

Birth involves the love hormone from the very beginning. Fetal lungs, when ready to breathe air, secrete surfactant components SP-A and PAF into the amniotic fluid in the mother's womb, causing the contractions of delivery to begin. The mother's body then produces oxytocin, stimulating more birth contractions. It's as if Mom says with her hormone language, "I can sense you are ready to breathe, so I will push you out and we can meet and cuddle."

Ordinarily a living thing coming out of our body would be a disgusting little parasitic horror needing to be tossed aside or killed, but a mother is programmed to trust the newborn coming out of her to be a friend, not a foe. It's literally a part of herself. At birth, a pact of trust is established. Through natural instincts the mother trusts that her baby is something to be cuddled and nurtured. The process begins during delivery as the baby moves through the cervix and vagina, which stimulates even more oxytocin synthesis to ready her to embrace her newborn. The baby then accepts its mother's affectionate touch for confirmation that it is welcomed into the world.

The first love a baby receives after birth is being held by its parents. When mom's hormones are messaging just right, the baby is irresistibly cute to her even if to no one else (though being born malformed may interfere with the impulse in our parents to cuddle). Newborns are pre-wired from birth to crave affectionate touch and to assume the person touching them is trustworthy as long it's a loving touch and not a painful touch.

Next is the mother's production of milk, also stimulated by oxytocin from the birth process and later from loving caresses and the baby's suckling. Part of the "trust" in the suckling act has to do with the assurance that the one suckling is, again, not eating her. The baby's instinct to suckle is an act of both taking and giving love. Taking, because the motions feel good to the baby, who also enjoys the sweet beverage, and *unknowingly giving love* to the mother receiving it via nerve endings in her nipples connected to brain centers and glands that produce for her pleasure and oxytocin. Nursing, when it's working like it is supposed to, is a mutual exchange of pleasure. Even so, suckling too aggressively by the baby can hurt the mother, and if she then pulls the baby off—denying the baby pleasure—the baby should eventually be able to learn to not suckle too hard, and the mother, hopefully, would be able to forgive her little one. In this way, because of the mother's feedback, the baby gets its first lesson in how to give and not just take love.

Cuddling and touching commences with family members and neighbors from the outset, and continues after weaning, although sibling rivalry can derail it. Children cuddle with parents, siblings, other relatives, pets and dolls as a normal healthy part of being in a family and growing up with loving habits. This has to shift somewhat in puberty, when the mating impulse comes into play. Then a stranger, usually outside of the family, becomes a primary affectionate companion. Again, the trust hormone oxytocin does its work of transforming a potential adversary from outside of the family into one to trust by expecting from them the pleasure of an intimate relationship rather than the fear of a stranger, rival, or outsider.

Mating is the ultimate form of loving trust because that's when adults have to overcome all their usual adversarial tendencies. Expectation of the intense pleasure of romantic companionship cancels out fear of rivalry and makes the relationship, at least temporarily though hopefully permanently, profoundly trusting. Lovers receive pleasure from each other through looks, smells, tastes, sounds, and touches. They exchange gazes of admiration, scents of hair and bodies, food and sweets, sighs and caresses. Lovers connect physically with sensitive and vulnerable parts of their bodies to show they trust they will not be injured there. In fact, those areas are especially sensitive to affection *because* they are vulnerable. Their sensitivity is to warn us to avoid being hurt, but in intimate lovemaking, to welcome the trustworthy, loving touch.

Lovers hold hands, hug, cuddle, and embrace, testing the willingness of their partner to return the touch and not to flinch or recoil. They kiss lips and skin, checking each other's tastes for health and genetic compatibility. Kissing and play-nibbling are expressions of confidence they won't be bitten. Even more so is tongue kissing, since putting one's tongue in another's mouth near their teeth shows profoundly confident trust. It's a non-verbal statement that says, "I trust you will not bite my tongue," which is answered by, "I will treat your tongue with care, proving to you I'm trustworthy" The act can be intensely pleasurable because of our basic craving to trust and be trusted. It's the way our DNA tells us "you should do this."

Other mating behaviors work the same way—dangerous contact with sensitive parts of our mates that communicate trust and trustworthiness are rewarded with intense pleasure. The neck is one of our vulnerable areas, since a bite there opening a jugular vein is efficiently fatal. But to a lover, we can present our neck for a kiss to show we know it won't be bitten, or for a hand that we know will not choke. Nipples can be a part of this, both men's and women's, because the suckling of lovers is an echo of the suckling of infants. Nipples are wired to our pleasure centers and are effective avenues of giving and receiving pleasure and signalling trust, both for infant suckling, and later, repurposed for adult lovemaking.

The ultimate in communicating trust in mating is how we treat each other's private parts. A lover can apply hands and mouth to our most sensitive and vulnerable parts with the understanding that we won't be injured there. The whole act of mating is, in summary, built on the understanding that we receive pleasure from our mates from the deep trust that they are good for us and will not hurt us, physically or emotionally.

In this way, our DNA provokes us to reproduce in a series of steps, each a pursuit of pleasure, that culminate in the appearance of the next generation.

Sleeping together, whether after intercourse or as a maturing family, is also a profound act of trust, since it shows one feels safe to be unconscious, and therefore completely defenseless, with someone else. If you fall asleep in another's arms, you show confidence you will wake up unharmed, and when you let someone sleep in your arms, you are inviting them to feel safe with you. The mutual, ultimate trust of sleeping together can therefore be astonishingly pleasurable.

Summary of this chapter:

1—We are born to love and be loved.

2—At each stage of our lives, the love instinct, based on the trust hormone oxytocin, regulates our connection with those we need for mutual survival in a cycle to repeat in the next generation.

I Love You Because You Hate Who I Hate

"The enemy of my enemy is my friend."
- Ancient proverb [9]

On holidays when I was young, my family visited our cousins and grandparents hundreds of miles away. Often, for no apparent reason, Grandma, a Slovakian immigrant, would bring up how awful Hitler was. She described ways she would torture him if she had the chance, even though he'd been dead for about twenty years. We all chimed in about what a horrible man he was. I think she seemed to know instinctively that disparaging someone not present (gossiping) would restore family affection weakened by us not having seen each other for half a year. Other targets of our shared condemnation included politicians, religious figures, comedians, modern musicians, abstract artists, or whomever. We needed to all agree who we didn't like so we could bind together once again in family affection via our shared disparagement.

There's an unfortunate irony in this, which is, disparaging others has the effect of enforcing love and affection. There's scientific support for this in recent studies that found unkind gossiping caused the affection hormone to be released (de Dreu, Greer, et al.). It makes sense, since group cohesion, trusting one another in a group, is necessary for staving off an enemy group. The problem this instinct causes has to do with the impulsiveness of choosing who we're going to regard as an enemy. "Us against them" triggers profound loss of empathy for whoever we happen, for the moment, to rally against, and it doesn't matter whether or not the disparaged ones deserve disparagement. Few really do. What's disconcerting is how much hatefulness is generated in this process of promoting affection. The million dollar question is, then, what's the net effect of this on the human condition?

Examples of alliances generated and supported by disparaging a common enemy:

Bosses against workers.
Workers against bosses.
Parents against their children.
Law enforcement officers against citizens.
Persecution of any demographic against another.
Sports teams against opposing teams and their fans.
Faith against faith.
Ideology against ideology.
Political rivalries.
Teachers against students.
Students against teachers.
Conformists against nonconformists.

It's quite limitless what examples of this can be included in the list. One thing that's amazing about the practice is how alliances can shift and flow from minute to minute. Let's take a hospital setting as an example. A patient may engage a nurse in disparaging the receptionist, hoping to make a connection with the nurse. Later in the day, the nurse and the receptionist may discuss their discontent with the new doctor on staff. Near the end of the day, that doctor and nurse discuss unhappiness with the building superintendent. The next day during lunch the whole staff might complain about a politician, who the patient at the beginning of this little saga thinks is a saint who will save us from that other political party the doctors and nurses have agreed to ally themselves with. In a day, a lot of hate'n to make a little love'n, and the love'n that comes from it can clearly be fleeting as alliances shift and flow. A quite unpleasant workplace can result from this kind of uncontrolled gossiping and disparagement.

The net effect of this syndrome, this habit, this ugly part of human nature, likely causes more discord than harmony, more misery than joy, more stress than comfort, and more hate than love.

A workaround for handling these kinds of ugly parts of human nature is to confine them to fantasy and play. Little harm is done to the real world if we get together at a *Star Wars* film and agree how bad Darth Vader is. Or, we can disparage sports teams in our effort to establish affinity with old and new friends. Historical figures? Why not? My grandmother's subtle intuitive wisdom of invoking family bonds by having us all agree on how awful long-dead Hitler was did the trick. Families can enjoy affectionate agreement about who the bad guys are as long as nobody gets hurt.

The next chapter covers other ways to make this world a more loving place.

Summary of this chapter:

1—We create momentary affection within a group by disparaging others.

2—The affection we create this way for the ingroup is likely less than the antagonism we make towards the outgroup which they also may direct back at us. It likely causes more hate'n than love'n.

3—Families and workplaces in which this syndrome is out of control will likely be unpleasant and inefficient, especially since unpredictable, shifting alliances can result in poor cooperation and even sabotage between individuals and groups.

4—We can avoid the spread of hatred by confining the gossip against common enemies to historical figures, characters of fiction, and opposing teams in game play.

Why Isn't There More Love in the World?

If it's such a great advantage to have trusted friends, family, and lovers, why does so much of the world seem like such an unloving, and at times, a downright hateful place? We are afraid of each other.

My brother liked to tell of his Indian coworker who asked him one day, "What does that mean, pushing up daisies? In India when we line up for the cinema, we place our hand on the shoulder of the person ahead of us. When I did this here in New York, I was warned to take my hand off or I'd be pushing up daisies." Yes, there's different tolerance for touching in different cultures—touching strangers, touching loved ones in public, and so forth, but it's telling that in some parts of Western culture, an innocent, unexpected touch instigated a death threat.

When we are starved of human contact, we crave it, but fear is holding us back. We could just get new friends, but we are too afraid to. That's why so many of us are alone. We are afraid of people we don't know, and they are afraid of us.

We are so afraid of each other that a child, sick with cancer and lonely in hospital isolation, cannot count on other humans for comfort and affection. How far we've wandered from nature if we are too afraid of each other to adequately comfort our sick and lonely. We give them animals—animals we've domesticated, in other words bred out of them what would terrify us if they were still in their original, undomesticated, predatory forms. We've bred dogs to give us love just like we've bred cows to give us milk and chickens to give us eggs. Why? Because we are too afraid of each other to give one another the love we need. In the most extreme cases, our fear of each other can be overwhelming, and we become trapped in a vicious cycle of loneliness and social rejection.

Because of our fear, we also seek affection from inert artifice. We leave children with stuffed toys. We engross ourselves in romantic fantasies on page and screen. Some men fill their homes with realistic or fantastical love dolls. Temple Grandin, an expert in the animal perspective of the world, because her social life's been hampered by her autism, developed a "hug box" she could retreat into for comfort. All this because, though we fear each other, our basic need for affection compels us to seek it from nonhuman or inanimate entities.

I was in high school at the onset of the Sexual Revolution in the late 60s. A Latin teacher, a spinster near retirement who'd never been married and reportedly lived alone with a little dog, assigned herself to be guardian of student sexual morality.

150

She watched the hallway during class breaks to force apart couples who were simply holding hands. Why did she do this? She was envious of those who had what she didn't have herself—real affection with another human being—and she was afraid of her own feelings of loneliness. Many kids just went on loving, dismissing her as a prudish fool. However, for some of the couples she separated, she planted a seed of shame—a fear of condemnation. These seeds of shame, once implanted and reinforced by others, can accumulate, fester, and sabotage relationships for life. This is likely what had happened to her. She'd been infected with shame, leaving her spouseless and childless, and she sought to infect others with her shame for needing affection.

Sexual prudishness, especially when it conflates nonsexual physical affection with sexuality, is but one of many reasons too many of us are starving for it and suffer from "skin hunger". Most of the time we are afraid of being used. There are a million ways we can be used by someone we give our affection and trust. We can be used sexually or financially, or dominated or targeted for emotional or physical cruelty. We can be trapped into relationships with people who, during courtship, had hidden parts of themselves that if we'd known of them, we would not have let them close (someone on their best behavior at the beginning of a friendship before their demons emerge). In the hormonal frenzy of new love we can be too easily seduced, ignoring warnings from real friends that "it's a trap," and fall for a Trojan Horse, a wolf in sheep's clothing, or simply a poor mate on their best behavior.

Nature deals us a faulty hand of cards, because, though as a group we do well if we cooperate, there's fleeting advantage in betrayal. The science of Game Theory shows why love must be cautious. The tit-for-tat model demonstrates that a group of individuals will do better if they cooperate with each other rather than compete. However, in a group of very nice people, a malicious individual can win great advantage for himself or herself. It can be the one who doesn't chip in at the lunch table, the Charlie Manson in the cuddly hippy commune, the one who never brings a dish to the pot luck, or the guy with AIDS at the orgy. The danger of trusting someone who shouldn't be trusted is, unfortunately, ever-present. We have good reason to fear betrayal, but when this fear is exaggerated, it can make for a very lonely world.

One of the reasons this book is important is that we often don't know what's bugging us and what we need to do to feel better. Say, if we're cranky from low blood sugar or dizzy from dehydration, we don't always recognize it as needing food or drink. Likewise, if we're miserable from a lack of positive social interactions, we may not know it's the reason we feel lousy or angry, and don't know how to overcome it. Instead, we attempt ultimately in vain to satisfy the hunger for companionship with animals, toys, fiction, and innumerable addictions. Even worse, we can, from lack of companionship, seek conflict and drama, self-defeatingly pushing others away and launching into a vicious cycle of escalating loneliness and depression.

Don't assume the friend-to-enemy ratio tends to always reach its natural balance. We can deliberately adjust our actions to build more and better friendships, more intimacy and more affection, and refuse to accept conflict that engenders a poisonous social environment. We have a chance at making this a more loving world if we see love as an integral part of nature, understandable through rational scientific inquiry, and manageable through knowledge and clear thinking.

Our children can be reminded how good trusting affection felt when they were younger and to be in the loving embrace of their mother, father, and family, and to endeavour to give that to anyone who can accept it—their brothers and sisters, friends and colleagues, lovers and spouses, children and grandchildren. We need more love in the world.

Summary:

1—Trust more, fear less.

2—Love is good, hate is bad.

Notes, References, and Further Reading

Carter C.S.; Ahnert L.; Grossmann K.; Hardy S.B.; Lamb M., Porges S.W.; Sachser N. (eds.) (2006). *Attachment and Bonding: A New Synthesis.* Cambridge, MA: MIT Press.

de Dreu, C.K.W.; L.L. Greer; S. Shalvi; M.J.J. Handgraaf; G.A. van Kleef; M. Baas; F.S. ten Velden; E. van Dijk; S.W.W. Feith: (2010). *The neuropeptide oxytocin regulates parochial altruism in intergroup conflict among humans. Science* (Vol. 328, no. 5984, p. 1343).

Dunbar, R. (2012). *The Science of Love.* Hoboken, NJ: John Wiley & Sons, Inc.

Floyd, Kory (2015). *The Loneliness Cure.* Avon, MA: Adams Media.

Fromm, E. (1956). *The Art of Loving.* New York, NY: Harper & Row.

Hari, J. (2015). *Chasing the Scream: The First and Last Days of the War on Drugs.* New York, NY: Bloomsbury USA.

Jackson, P. (2013). *Eleven Rings: The Soul of Success.* New York, NY: The Penguin Press.

Kimes, M. (2013). *At Sears, Eddie Lampert's Warring Divisions Model Adds to the Troubles.* New York, NY: Bloomberg.

Sapolsky, R. M. (2004). *Why Zebras Don't Get Ulcers.* New York, NY: Henry Holt and Company.

Sapolsky, R. M. (2010). *Human Biology 106 Lecture Series.* Stanford, CA: Stanford University YouTube Channel.

Sapolsky, R. M. (2017). *Behave: The Biology of Humans at Our Best and Worst.* New York, NY: Penguin Press.

Stoller, K. P. (2012). *Oxytocin: The Hormone of Healing and Hope.* Middletown, DE: Dream Treader Press.

Szalavitz, M. (2016). *Unbroken Brain: A Revolutionary New Way of Understanding Addiction.* New York, NY: St. Martin's Press.

Zak, P. J. (2012). *The Moral Molecule: The Source of Love and Prosperity.* New York, NY: Dutton.

Sources of Quotations

1 - Taylor, Jeremy, 1613-1667, Cleric of the Church of England.

2 - Roberts, A. (1944) *You Always Hurt the One You Love* (song title).

3 - Diderot, D. (1749). *Letter on the Blind for the Use of Those Who Can See.*

4 - Krause, L., Baggini, J. (2012). *Philosophy v Science: Which Can Answer the Big Questions of Life?* London, UK: Guardian Media Group plc. Used with permission.

5 - Laozi (c 531 BC). *Tao Te Ching.* China.

6 - Wilde, O. (1891). *The Picture of Dorian Gray.* London, UK: Simpkin, Marshall, Hamilton, Kent & Co., Ltd.

7 - Humes, H. (1971). Private conversations. Princeton, NJ.

8 - Penn, William. *Fruits of Solitude. Vol. I, Part 3.* The Harvard Classics. New York: P.F. Collier & Son, 1909–14

9 - Traditional.

www.ingramcontent.com/pod-product-compliance
Lightning Source LLC
Chambersburg PA
CBHW030250030426
42336CB00009B/326